Advanc

MW01611685

"Cesi's plays are adventures in wordscapes that show us the ways we are and the ways we can be. Characters not often seen on screen, stage or page populate her scenes in situations that make these short plays eminently readable and relatable while being unapologetically unique. Lovers of theater and fiction alike will find much to cherish in this collection. Bravo!"

   —Celeste Rita Baker, Author of *Back, Belly and Side*

"Cesi Davidson's delightful and wise, *Articulation: Short Plays to Nourish Mind and Soul* illuminates the human condition. Her method: create non human beings ranging from those plucked from nursery rhymes to celestial beings to fruits, vegetables and animals and put them in distinctly human situations like Bo Peep losing her sheep because her husband sold them to bet on horses. What makes these plays particularly satisfying is Davidson's ability to weave tough-minded outcomes like lost sheep and street violence with sympathetic characters and sly humor."

   —Daniel Judah Sklar. DJS, playwright, author of *Playmaking: Children Writing & Performing Their Own Plays*— Distinguished Book Award from The American Alliance for Theater & Education.

"In this collection, Cesi Davidson presents work that draws fantasy, fairy tale and fun to grapple with many human situations. A bird or a bunny or a banana may have dialogue in her stories as frequently as human characters. You never can predict the form of her storytelling, but you will always be moved."

   —Martha Wade Steketee, Research, Criticism, Dramaturgy, www.urbanexcavations.com

"Cesi Davidson's short plays are swift but indelible, both light and enlightening, their profound human truths conveyed with power and originality. Each piece assembles an intriguing, often whimsical or fantastic cast of characters (a young man and his dream mothers, two guardians standing watch on a pregnant woman's belly, a ripening banana and its peel…) and gives them unbridled voice. The result is a series of interactions that embody fresh takes on the conundrums, the alienations and vulnerabilities—including those of race and class and gender and sexuality—of contemporary life. We're awakened to our own ability to express our experiences, to feel our pain and that of others, to persevere."

—John Gould, Author of the Giller Prize shortlisted *Kilter: 55 Fictions*

"Intricate…at times humorous, at turns complex and serious. These are the short plays of an incredibly deft playwright. Cesi Davidson is a keen observer of human behavior and social issues juxtaposing fairy tales with twenty first century life, dreams weaving in and through time as well as social unrest and harmony. Some conjure up a painful history imbued with deep compassion and a questioning by the viewer of 'where do we go from here?' A few of them remind me of the great Harold Pinter and others in their playful absurdity bring to mind Ionesco. All are packed with a twist—a zag where you might expect a zig. Good art inspires personal and collective introspection and deep thought as well as joy. These plays certainly deliver."

—Whitney Hamilton, Playwright/Screenwriter/novelist Bjornquistfilms.com

"SEE CESI DANCE...
And the African joy of old
Lights the room
Open this Book
And you might find yourself
In a world where radish have souls
AND TALK
OR In a realm where
Purity percentage of truth in Love
Is the currency
For longevity in Life
Where writers fly...Daily
And actors become borderless
OPEN THIS BOOK
AND ride the WORDWAVES
OF 'The Lorraine Hansberry' of our time!"

—Kene Holliday, Actor...Director...Writer: Private
Investigator, Tyler Hudson... *MATLOCK*...TV
Jazz Soprano Saxophonist Sydney Bechet...
THE JOSEPHINE BAKER STORY... FILM
Sargent Curtis Baker ... *Carter Country*... TV Series

ARTICULATION

Conversation Pieces

A Small Paperback Series from Aqueduct Press
Subscriptions available: www.aqueductpress.com

About the Aqueduct Press
Conversation Pieces Series

The feminist engaged with sf is passionately interested in challenging the way things are, passionately determined to understand how everything works. It is my constant sense of our feminist-sf present as a grand conversation that enables me to trace its existence into the past and from there see its trajectory extending into our future. A genealogy for feminist sf would not constitute a chart depicting direct lineages but would offer us an ever-shifting, fluid mosaic, the individual tiles of which we will probably only ever partially access. What could be more in the spirit of feminist sf than to conceptualize a genealogy that explicitly manifests our own communities across not only space but also time?

Aqueduct's small paperback series, Conversation Pieces, aims to both document and facilitate the "grand conversation." The Conversation Pieces series presents a wide variety of texts, including short fiction (which may not always be sf and may not necessarily even be feminist), essays, speeches, manifestoes, poetry, interviews, correspondence, and group discussions. Many of the texts are reprinted material, but some are new. The grand conversation reaches at least as far back as Mary Shelley and extends, in our speculations and visions, into the continually created future. In Jonathan Goldberg's words, "To look forward to the history that will be, one must look at and retell the history that has been told." And that is what Conversation Pieces is all about.

L. Timmel Duchamp

Jonathan Goldberg, "The History That Will Be" in Louise Fradenburg and Carla Freccero, eds., *Premodern Sexualities* (New York and London: Routledge, 1996)

Conversation Pieces
Volume 71

ARTICULATION
Short Plays to Nourish the Mind & Soul

by
Cesi Davidson

Published by Aqueduct Press
PO Box 95787
Seattle, WA 98145-2787
www.aqueductpress.com

ISBN: 978-1-61976-175-9

Cover illustration courtesy Michal Ammar
Veronica Bunny illustrations courtesy Ayumi Nakao
Dream Mother illustration (p. 15) courtesy Noriko Sugiura
Voice Lessons illustration (p. 102) courtesy Michal Ammar

Original Block Print of Mary Shelley by Justin Kempton:
www.writersmugs.com

Printed in the USA by Applied Digital Imaging

Acknowledgments

My sister Cheryl told me I was funny. When it became apparent that I should write plays, I asked my cousin Mickey, a dancer and choreographer, for advice about next steps. She guided me to Woody King Jr.'s New Federal Theatre. Later, when I ventured uptown in New York City, I connected with Eddie Pomerantz and the Harlem Dramatic Writers. I valued the opportunities to write and share. My sister friend Celeste held my hand as I walked the sidewalks of Harlem looking for a nest to present my work. In the by and by, Celeste and her husband Richard Baker created a Harlem Renaissance Salon in their living room where actor's read my plays. In the milieu of Richard's visual art, and with snacks and beverages, neighbors, friends, and fans found delight in listening to my stories. My sidewalk strolling for a more permanent home ended at the George Bruce Library. This New York Public Library, under the visionary leadership of Junelle Carter Bowman, recognized and embraced the importance of building a free public program for culturally responsive theatre in a neighborhood environment. Home Sweet Soulful Home. I made this enduring pledge to the audience:

You're invited after work, before dinner, after dinner, before the gym, after homework with the kids, on the way home, as you get off the bus, a few extra subway stops, or a short cab ride, for an hour of theatre. The price of admission is only your authentic self. You'll hear plays that will excite you, delight you, surprise you, heal you, soothe you, validate you, help you question, tickle your funny bone, scream with you, and perhaps kiss you goodnight. Leave your drama and enjoy our drama.

Many directors, actors, musicians, and dancers released their sweat birthing my plays. Here they are:

Andrea Abello, Alvin Alexis, Lauren Annunziata, Elizabeth Acosta, Miriam Agwai, Segun Akande, Abraham Amkpa, Alva Anderson, E. J. An, Tonia Anderson, Charese Annel, April Armstrong, Maitefa Angaza, Celeste Rita Baker, Marie Barrientos, Gregory Bastien, James Edward Becton, Lucia Bellini, Sara Berg, Collin Biddle, Alex Blade Silver, Husani Blaze, Johnny Blaze Leavitt, Monica Blaze Leavitt, Paul Bolger, Cate Bottiglione, Philip Burke, Amara Brady, Laurabeth Breya, David Brooks, Soraya Broukhim, Jordan Brown, Charles Brice, Vinie Burrows, Christine Campbell, Trevania Campbell, Kenya Capers, Daniel Carlton, Marlon Carter, Natalie Carter, Amanda Cannon, Don Castro, Jill Chenault, Michael Chenevert, Kim Chinh, Marie Cisco, Michael Citriniti, Shamira Clark, Ginnine Cocuzza, Sabrina Colie, China L. Colston, Ashelee Danielle, Clea DeCrane, Sandra A. Daley-Sharif, Billy Davis, Elaine Davis, Andre Dell, William Duffy, Ariel Dupas, Tonya Edmonds, Pierre Edouard, Charles Edward, Matthew Faroul, Sidiki Fofana, Matthew Faroul, Brent Fayzon, Jose Febus, Michael Flood, Patricia Floyd, Jeannine Foster-McKelvia, Bruce Fuller, Aaron Fried, Xavier Galva, Nimo Gandhi, Hope Garland, Keith Gittens, Letitia Guillory, Marie Guiner, Michael Anthony Green, Tiffany Nicole Greene, Zaria Griffin, Tristan Halstead, Felicia Harden-Bradford, Lorna Haughton, Mike Hodge, Fulton C. Hodges, Mary Hodges, Kene Holiday, Bryan Henao, Sharon Hope, Denise Allesandra Hurd, Mateo Hurtado, Daralyn Jay, Cara Jaye, Ralph Emerson John, Marjorie Johnson, Melissa Joyner, Sandra Kazan, Nambi E. Kelley, Joy Kelly, Axia Kendrick, Sean Kenin, Ariel Kim, Carolyn Kitay, Starr Kirkland, Cassagnol Leonides Jr., Sara Kiefer,

Brad Lewandowski, Sharon Lynn, Kathryn Long, Justin Lord, Clinton Lowe, Leopold Lowe, Rachel Lu, Julie Ann Lucas, Shereen Macklin, Jamil Mangan, Chenana Manno, Tom Martin, Dara Marsh, Thea Martinez, Johnnie Mae, Alisha Danielle May, Kellie McCants, Arlene A. McGruder, Jasper McGruder, Sharon McGruder, Isreal McKinney Scott, Susan McWilliams, Qaasim Middleton, Harry Miller, Vernice Miller, Sandra Mills Scott, Jomack Miranda, Ivan Moore, Pamela Monroe, Khemali Murray, Sam Morales, Mansoor Najee-ullah, Marie Elena O'Brien, Sheila Joon Ostadazim, Caitlin Perez, Dominican Pie, Ashton Pina, Tonya Pinkins, Reynaldo Piniella, Cassie Post, Beverly Prentice Campbell, Doris Kay Prester, Alex Purcell, Jerome Preston, Marsha Regis, Torre Reigns, Alize Rejouis, Sarina Renee, Chaz Reuben, Joanna Rhinehart, Gha'il Rhodes Benjamin, Melissa Riker, Clea Rivera, David Roberts, Judith Roberts, Betsy Rosen, Toni Seawright, Krystal Seli, Tracy Shar, Lauren Schaffel, Brent Shultz, Claire Simba, Norman Anthony Small, Nzingtha Smith, Tarantino Smith, Paola A. Soto, Johndca Spencer, Kevin Stanfa, Illana Stein, Gloria Strauss, LeVera Sutton, Jennifer Terrell, chandra thomas, Rosita Timm, Myxy Tyler, Joyce Sylvester, Charles Turner, Joan Valentina, Gary Vincent, Althea Alexis Vyfhuis, Douglas Wade, Jak Watson, William Oliver Watkins, Najuma Weeks, Keona Welch, Patricia White, Jared Wilder, Iris Wilson, David D. Wright, Gameela Wright, Yan Xi, and James Zebooker.

The audience makes theatre possible. My dear audiences brought warmth, acceptance, and love. Thank you for the love. I love you back.
Cesi Davidson, September 2019

For all I am and hope to become, I'm indebted to my parents Charles and Florence Davidson.

Contents

FOREWORD

by Zachary Sklar
Oscar-nominated screenwriter for JFK
(with Oliver Stone)

Prolific and visionary, Cesi Davidson is a unique artist. In less than a decade, she has written and produced more than two hundred Short Plays to Nourish the Mind and Soul. Some of Cesi's plays have been performed in Off Off Broadway theaters. As of 2019, her plays are in the fifth season of free dramatic readings at public libraries in New York City's Harlem community. Wildly imaginative, funny, disturbing, and touching, these plays have inspired an ongoing dialogue with Harlem residents about personal, political, and spiritual issues affecting individual lives and the collective life of the community. Cesi's work, though still evolving, has already carved out an important niche and made a major contribution to Harlem's legendary cultural tradition.

I first met Cesi seven years ago when she joined the Harlem Dramatic Writing Workshop, founded more than two decades ago by Edward Pomerantz and the Writers Guild East to offer free classes to adult Harlem writers. I was leading the screenwriting section, and Cesi wanted to adapt one of her plays into a movie. Quiet, intelligent, and sensitive, Cesi had a sharp ear for dialogue and a fresh imagination bursting with ideas.

Cesi found a medium for her work in the Short Playwriting section led by Eddie Pomerantz. In the workshop's Playmaking section, led by Daniel Sklar, she further developed her own singular voice.

The outpouring of imaginative energy that followed was truly astonishing. With a full-time job and family responsibilities, Cesi awakened every day at 3 a.m. to write for several hours creating plays at a rapid pace. Cesi's work is not only prolific, but also wide-ranging in scope. And her remarkable productivity shows no signs of slowing down.

In these fanciful, often hilarious plays you will discover a fantastic variety of characters—familiar nursery-rhyme figures who work in a ninety-nine-cent store and bet on horses, bananas and radishes, who discuss their ill-fated destinies, birds who sing songs of unrequited love, time travelers who skip about from the Caribbean present-day to slavery-era Virginia, bunnies who meet in support groups.

Many of the plays will have you laughing out loud. But they also explore serious issues and wrenching troubles. Little Bo Peep finds her marriage destroyed by the gambling habits of Big Man Blue. A bunny mother struggles to accept her gender-fluid son/daughter. A young man dreams of different incarnations of his drug-addicted mother, hoping for maternal love to conquer his pain. A traumatized African-American woman seeks to wash away the bloody stains of a racially motivated violent assault.

Cesi Davidson's plays are intended as metaphors to stir our emotions and provoke our thoughts. For those who haven't had the pleasure of seeing the plays in person, now this book provides a sampling of the exciting experience audiences have enjoyed and hopefully will continue to enjoy for years to come. Savor these plays. They offer true nourishment for the mind and soul.

INTRODUCTION

I entered the world of dramatic writing unexpectedly but universe aligned. My career has centered around one focus: speech and language pathology; facilitating human development and the ability of individuals to communicate. Listen. Speak. Read. Write. I've been privileged to experience the vastness of individual triumphs and suffering. In the process, I've discovered that conversation is critical. It supports our socialization and uplifts us into our humanity. How fortuitous that my first venture into an anthology of my own writing should be published in a series entitled Conversation Pieces. I'm forever grateful to Aqueduct Press for including my work in their series.

Real life conversation requires a speaker and a listener. In the midst of our human struggles, we often forget that communication is a shared activity, the goal of which is to exchange meaning. Human beings, unlike computer programs, are physically unable to articulate exactly the same way every time. We are simply perfectly imperfect. That's okay. Rapid technology-mediated encounters, screen-to-screen interactions, and abbreviated texting seldom capture full intentions, emotionality, and truth.

A play lovingly forces us to live the moments of dialogue between characters. It gently forces perspective taking. We can live in worlds real and imaged. The events in the worlds advance through words triggering actions and actions triggering words. Reading and imagining the life of the play is pure freedom. The drama can become a rehearsal for life.

My dear reader, my wish is that you'll read these plays in whatever way suits your mood and fancy. Each play represents an individual exploration of a story. Enjoy. And when you're finished, I'll have more for you. I offer you this taste.

Cesi
September 2019

NURSERY RHYMES IN THE NINETY-NINE II

Sweetable Cheatable

Characters

Little Bo Peep: Sheepherder, storekeeper, married to Big Man Blue

Big Man Blue: Freelance horn player, gambler, married to Little Bo Peep

Setting

Rhyme Town. A "parallel world" inside the Village of Harlem. Interior of Little Bo Peep and Big Man Blue's home. A ninety-nine cent store is on the ground level. Little Bo Peep is doing various storekeeping tasks including arranging merchandise, and counting money in the cash register. She frequently looks out of the windows.

(Lights Rise)
(Enter Big Man Blue carrying a newspaper.)

LITTLE BO PEEP: Where've you been Blue?

BIG MAN BLUE: Over on Sugar Hill.

3

LITTLE BO PEEP: With whom?

BIG MAN BLUE: Jack.

LITTLE BO PEEP: It's close to sundown. What were you and Jack doing together on Sugar Hill at this hour?

BIG MAN BLUE: Peep! You're asking me about my business. I don't like you asking me about my business.

LITTLE BO PEEP: You were supposed to help me with the inventory in the store. I have to go watch the kids for the Old Woman in the Shoe later. I can't finish the inventory today by myself.

BIG MAN BLUE: Finish it tomorrow.

LITTLE BO PEEP: It needs to get finished today. I have to place orders.

BIG MAN BLUE: I got caught up with things.

LITTLE BO PEEP: You're always "caught up."

BIG MAN BLUE: (Making notes on his newspaper.) The inventory doesn't matter.

LITTLE BO PEEP: What did you say?

BIG MAN BLUE: I'll help you in a few minutes.

LITTLE BO PEEP: Why was Jack with you?

(Pause)

He should have been helping Jill fetch some water.

BIG MAN BLUE: (Reading the paper)
Hey diddle the cat and the fiddle, the cow jumped over the moon...

LITTLE BO PEEP: Blue?

BIG MAN BLUE: They have their own marriage, and what they do is between them. Always in somebody's business Peep.

LITTLE BO PEEP: Jill's my friend.

BIG MAN BLUE: And Jack's my friend. I don't tell him how to handle his wife, and he doesn't tell me how to handle mine.

LITTLE BO PEEP: Jill has arthritis now. It's too painful for her to fetch water by herself and carry pails up and down Sugar Hill. Jack needs to help her.

BIG MAN BLUE: And you need to stay out of it.

LITTLE BO PEEP: Does Jill know her new pails came in?

BIG MAN BLUE: I didn't see her.

LITTLE BO BEEP: I hope she's okay.

(Looking out of the windows more intensely)

I ordered some special pails for her. They're made for lefties out of this new plastic material...very light weight. It'll take some stress off her shoulders and her back. The colors are so pretty...bright pastels. I thought the colors would help her feel happy.

BIG MAN BLUE: What did you make for my dinner?

LITTLE BO PEEP: Have you seen the sheep?

BIG MAN BLUE: (Drawing the curtains on the windows)
No.

LITTLE BO PEEP: Leave the curtains open. There's still some daylight. And I want to keep an eye out for the sheep…they should have been home from the meadow by now.

BIG MAN BLUE: I don't want Peeping Tom looking through the windows.

LITTLE BO PEEP: (Opening the curtains again)
Tom is harmless. He's just curious. Besides, there's nothing going on in here worth looking at.

(Exit to kitchen.)

BIG MAN BLUE: (On the phone)
Little Pig? Yeah… It's Big Man Blue. I want you to put one thousand Rhyme Town bit coins on All the King's Horses and All the King's Men to win. Yeah, I'm good for it…came into some cash… Besides, I'll be picking up cash from you later after the race. Jack tipped me. This is gonna pay off big.

(Enter Little Bo Peep.)

LITTLE BO PEEP: The pudding and pie is almost ready.

BIG MAN BLUE: I'm sick of eating pudding and pie.

LITTLE BO PEEP: Georgie Porgie is stopping by.

BIG MAN BLUE: I don't want him over here anymore.

LITTLE BO PEEP: He's bringing over some photographs to show me from his trip with Puss 'n Boots.

BIG MAN BLUE: I said, "No."

LITTLE BO PEEP: He's just a friend, Blue. Can't I have any friends over, Blue?

BIG MAN BLUE: Sure. Little Miss Muffet... Invite Jill over...since you're so concerned about her. I'm eating out...I'll pick up a sandwich with Old King Cole at the castle.

LITTLE BO PEEP: Is that really where you're going? Let's not pretend, Blue. You were on the phone with one of the pigs, weren't you?

BIG MAN BLUE: (Arranging pails on the shelves) I'll help with some inventory before I leave. These are the pails for Jill? You can't charge ninety-nine cents for these. You need to mark up the prices.

LITTLE BO PEEP: This is a ninety-nine cents store. Everything needs to cost ninety-nine cents.

BIG MAN BLUE: And up. The sign on the store needs to say, "And Up." We keep around a few things that cost ninety-nine cents, but we make our money on the big-ticket items...up to ninety-nine dollars.

LITTLE BO PEEP: We never got into this business to cheat other nursery rhyme characters.

BIG MAN BLUE: Making money is not cheating.

LITTLE BO PEEP: Nursery rhyme characters our age have fixed incomes. They can't afford to pay outrageous prices for basic necessities.

BIG MAN BLUE: Which reminds me. Tell your friend Little Miss Muffet she needs to pay up her tab for the curds and whey.

LITTLE BO PEEP: She's having a hard time right now. Just diagnosed with diabetes.

BIG MAN BLUE: Not our problem. If she weren't sitting on her tuffet all day getting fat, maybe she wouldn't be sick.

LITTLE BO PEEP: (Looking out of the windows as she sings)
Brooklyn Bridge is falling down, falling down, falling down
Brooklyn Bridge is falling down, my fair lady.

Take the keys and lock them up, lock them up, lock them up
Take the keys and lock them up. My fair lady.

BIG MAN BLUE: You haven't sung that song in a long time.

LITTLE BO PEEP: I haven't felt this way in a long time, or maybe I haven't wanted to admit it. Feeling hopeless…locked up. Let's not pretend.

BIG MAN BLUE: We're nursery rhyme characters… it's all about pretending.

LITTLE BO PEEP: You were on the phone with one of the three little pigs, weren't you?

BIG MAN BLUE: Why are you asking if you know?

LITTLE BO PEEP: Which one was it?
(Pause)
Which one?

BIG MAN BLUE: The one with the straw house.

LITTLE BO PEEP: The Big Bad Wolf is gonna to huff and puff and blow his house down and all of our money will be flying to every corner of Rhyme Town.

BIG MAN BLUE: You're exaggerating. Not gonna happen.

LITTLE BO PEEP: He's a bad pig. He was in the forest with the Big Bad Wolf when that poor little girl, Little Red Riding Hood was abducted on her way to grandma's house. All they ever found was a basket full of goodies. It's just a matter of time before the Big Bad Wolf...

BIG MAN BLUE: I don't owe you an explanation Peep.

LITTLE BO PEEP: I'm your wife. Do you owe me anything Blue?

BIG MAN BLUE: This time, the tip is gonna pay off. We're gonna win big. Jack got a new source.

LITTLE BO PEEP: (Looking out of the window)
The sun's down. The sheep aren't back. You're not worried?
(Pause)
How did you get the money to give to the pig?
(Pause)
You're not going to the castle...you're going to the

Hey Diddle Race Track. How did you get money for the bet?

BIG MAN BLUE: I sold the sheep. We didn't need them. You didn't need them. You retired from sheep herding. They were more mouths to feed, taking up space, eating all the grass in the meadow.

LITTLE BO PEEP: Get them back.

BIG MAN BLUE: It's done, Bo Peep.

LITTLE BO PEEP: Bring my sheep home.

BIG MAN BLUE: I sold them to the butcher. They're muttonchops by now.

LITTLE BO PEEP: My sheep…my poor sheep… slaughtered…you take every joy I have… When you lost your own joy…playing your horn…you started chipping away every part of my world… everything that made me happy.

(Big Man Blue gathers a few things and prepares to leave.)

BIG MAN BLUE: *On the field the shepherd boy*
Calling for his sheep
Plays this tune upon his horn
Calling them to sleep
Loo, loo, loo, loo
Loo, loo, loo, loo, loo
Bad ass jammin with that tune back in the day. Blowing til sunrise…

LITTLE BO PEEP: It was your tune that called me. I fell in love with you first through your tune. Cool Blue.

BIG MAN BLUE: *Loo, loo, loo, loo, loo*

LITTLE BO PEEP: You could get down.

BIG MAN BLUE: Then the gigs for horn players dried up in Rhyme Town.

LITTLE BO PEEP: You never needed a gig for an excuse to play your tunes.

BIG MAN BLUE: Humpty... When Humpty Dumpty fell off the wall and shattered into pieces something inside me shattered too, and I couldn't put myself together again. You could never understand what that means to be so shattered inside that you're lost from yourself.

LITTLE BO PEEP: I do. We're not good for each other, Blue.

(Pause)

I'll pack a few of your things that you'll need right away. I'll send them to the Grimm Brothers.

BIG MAN BLUE: The Grimm brothers are on the other side of the enchanted forest. No nursery rhyme characters there.

LITTLE BO PEEP: There needs to be some distance between us. Maybe you can find yourself again, living with fairy tales. I can't hold on to you anymore. Holding on to you means letting go of me. Send for the rest of your things when you get settled. Try the wicked witch. She may have a cottage to rent. You should take your horn. Maybe you'll find the soul to play tunes again.

BIG MAN BLUE: I'm not going anywhere. You need me.

LITTLE BO PEEP: I need, no, I want, a nursery rhyme man who loves and cares for me. You sold my sheep. That man isn't you anymore. I've been walking on the edge of fantasy and reality with you for a long time.

BIG MAN BLUE: This is my house. I'm not going anywhere.

LITTLE BO PEEP: It was always your home. It was never your house. Mother Goose made sure of that.

BIG MAN BLUE: Why are you bringing up your mother?

LITTLE BO PEEP: She put my name on the deed for the store and the house. Only my name. I own this place.

BIG MAN BLUE: She wouldn't do that.

LITTLE BO PEEP: She would, and she did. Mother Goose told me, even women who are happy in a marriage should have an exit strategy. It's kind of like insurance. No nursery rhyme woman should feel locked up with a key.
(Pause)
Shouldn't you be getting to the racetrack?

BIG MAN BLUE: Yeah, and then I'll be back. You can't make me go.

LITTLE BO PEEP: I have some other insurance.

BIG MAN BLUE: What?

LITTLE BO PEEP: Georgie Porgie.

(Lights Out)

End of Play

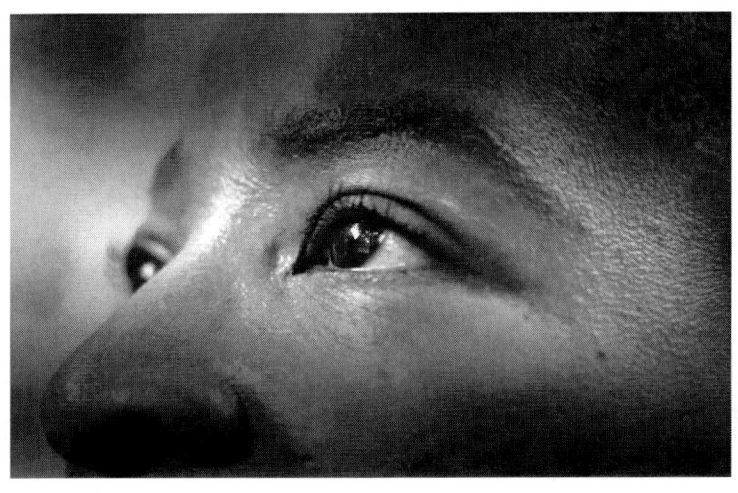

DREAM MOTHER

Riding to the Other Side of Love

Characters

Brendan Brown: Twenty-something man

Dream Mother One: Female subway passenger

Dream Mother Two: Female subway passenger

Dream Mother Three: Female subway passenger

Dream Mother Four: Female subway passenger/
Rehabilitation Counselor

Setting

The present. Morning. Number Six local subway train
traveling from the Bronx to Manhattan. Brendan and
all passengers are seated, waiting for their subway stops.

VOICE: This is the Number Six train. Watch the
closing doors.

(Sound Effect: Subway doors closing)

(Dream Mother One and Brendan step to adjacent subway
straps. They look at each other and then look forward.)

DREAM MOTHER ONE: Brendan Brown, come over here. You gonna stand here with me until I tell you to go. Where in hell is Ronald? He shoulda been here by now. Get over there to the corner and keep lookin out. Make sure nobody else is comin.

BRENDAN: Mom…I need to get to school.

DREAM MOTHER ONE: Shut up… Keep lookin out.

BRENDAN: Mom…I'm hungry…

DREAM MOTHER ONE: Are you lookin out like I told you, boy? Damn it… Where is Ronald… I need my stuff… He promised to give me a little…

BRENDAN: Mom… If I'm late, I'll miss the school breakfast.

DREAM MOTHER ONE: Then you'll eat the free lunch.

BRENDAN: My class has the late lunch period. I'll have to wait until 1:30 to eat.

DREAM MOTHER ONE: Are you crying?

(Dream Mother One slaps Brendan.)

Now you have something to cry about. Where's the money you been getting from Junior's Barber Shop?

BRENDAN: I don't know.

DREAM MOTHER ONE: You need another one across your face, Brendan? Junior told me he gives you five dollars every day after school to sweep up the cut hair.

(Brendan reaches into his shoe.)

16

BRENDAN: I want to save it.

(Dream Mother One snatches the money.)

DREAM MOTHER ONE: You ain't got nothing that isn't mine, Brendan. I brought you into this world.

(Pause)

Whatcha lookin at me for?

BRENDAN: I need the money. I want to go on the class trip.

DREAM MOTHER ONE: I need it more. Nice stash you been holdin out on your mother, you little ungrateful... Go on, get to school and don't come home before seven... I'm gonna be takin care my business.

BRENDAN: If I don't have a note for being late, I'll get detention.

DREAM MOTHER ONE: Detention? Then don't go to school. I don't give a damn, Brendan. You're such an odd person. *"I want breakfast." "I want my money." "I'll get detention."* I don't know how I ended up with a punk- ass crybaby. I don't think you're mine. Mix up at the hospital maybe... Get outta my face.

(Sound Effect: Subway doors open)

VOICE: Next stop Yankee Stadium.

(Dream Mother One exits. Dream Mother Two enters and stands next to Brendan.)

Watch the closing doors.

(Dream Mother Two and Brendan look at each other and then look forward.)

17

DREAM MOTHER TWO: What's my surprise, Brendan?

BRENDAN: It's a secret, Mom.

DREAM MOTHER TWO: No secrets. I'm excited.

(Sound Effects: James Brown: I Feel Good)

BRENDAN: Okay Mom, close your eyes and then open them.

(Brendan sings and dances to music.)

DREAM MOTHER TWO: You're doing our happy dance.

(Dream Mother Two opens her eyes and sings and dances with Brendan. Brendan shows his mother a document.)

BRENDAN: I got in, Mom. A full scholarship.

DREAM MOTHER TWO: Oh my God… Oh my God…I'm so proud of you.

BRENDAN: This is one of the top high schools in the country… And they pay for everything. And look at this Mom… They have a real football field and tennis courts and a pool and a swim club ,.and a real lab for science experiments. I get to stay in a house with house parents.

DREAM MOTHER TWO: House parents?

BRENDAN: They're not real parents. They just call them that because they help you like a parent would at home. You're my real mother and my father… Nothing changes that…

DREAM MOTHER TWO: This isn't a dream anymore… A good school… It's so far away, Brendan…

BRENDAN: They pay for me to come home during all of the school holidays. And I can write you every day.

DREAM MOTHER TWO: Write me? Can you call me every day?

BRENDAN: I don't know. They have a lot of rules, strict… They want students to concentrate on learning and not have any distractions.

DREAM MOTHER TWO: I'm your mother… I'm not a distraction.

BRENDAN: No… They mean the other stuff…

(Pause)

You want me to go, right Mom?

DREAM MOTHER TWO: Yes… I want you to go… This is a dream come true… This is your opportunity, your chance that you can't miss. I know you can't get much from these schools around here…

BRENDAN: Will you be all right without me, Mom?

DREAM MOTHER TWO: Will I be all right? Who is the grown-up here?

BRENDAN: I mean… You know…

DREAM MOTHER TWO: That doesn't happen anymore.

(She sings)

I feel good…

BRENDAN: I feel good too, Mom. Thank you.

VOICE: Next stop One Hundred Thirty-Eighth Street and the Grand Concourse. Connections here for New York City Bronx Court Detention Facilities.

(Sound Effect: Subway doors closing)

(Dream Mother Two exits. Dream Mother Three enters. Brendan and Dream Mother Three look at each other and then look forward.)

BRENDAN: Where are you taking my mother?

DREAM MOTHER THREE: Get off me.

BRENDAN: Leave her alone. You're hurting her.

DREAM MOTHER THREE: Ronald. Where's my shoes? Let me get my shoes, damn it. These cuffs are too tight.

BRENDAN: She's sick. She needs a hospital. You're hurting her.

DREAM MOTHER THREE: Who the hell are you? Ronald! Let me call Ronald… He can straighten this out.

(Pause)

Wait…Ronald… That's him over there… It was jus… It was jus… I jus wanted what he promised me. It was a mistake… I jus wanted what he promised me, and he was holdin out… It went off by itself... I was only tryin to scare him... Make him give me my stuff...

BRENDAN: I'll get you some help, Mom. Don't worry...

DREAM MOTHER THREE: Who the hell are you?

BRENDAN: I'm Brendan, Mom, your son.

DREAM MOTHER THREE: My son is gone...he left me.

(Dream Mother Three exits. Dream Mother Four stands next to Brendan. They look at each other and then look forward.)

VOICE: Because of police activity, the last and final stop on this train will be One hundred and Twenty Fifth Street. All exit...next stop One Hundred Twenty Fifth Street.

(Sound Effect: Subway doors open)

(Dream Mother Four and Brendan then exit in opposite directions.)

Setting

Drug Rehabilitation Center

DREAM MOTHER FOUR/REHABILITATION COUNSELOR: Your mother refuses to see you. I'm sorry. We can't force visitation.

(Brendan gives a CD and bouquet of flowers to the counselor.)

BRENDAN: Give her these, please.

REHABILITATION COUNSELOR: A James Brown CD?

BRENDAN: It has some music that she used to like. Maybe she'll remember.

(Brendan turns to exit.)

REHABILITATION COUNSELOR: She keeps the flowers.

(Brendan turns around.)

Every month you bring her flowers, and she keeps them after they're old and dried up.

BRENDAN: That's good.

REHABILITATION COUNSELOR: She told me she wouldn't throw the flowers away unless all the life in them was gone.

(Brendan turns to exit.)

REHABILITATION COUNSELOR: Why do you keep coming? Do you believe she'll want to see you one day?

BRENDAN: I see her every day. She's my dream mother. I come here for me, so I can keep remembering to love. If I can't love anymore, then nothing I own, nothing I've accomplished, is worth it.

(Brendan turns to exit.)

REHABILITATION COUNSELOR: Can you wait a few minutes?

(Brendan turns around.)

REHABILITATION COUNSELOR: I can take my coffee break soon. We can...

BRENDAN: Maybe another time...

(Brendan pulls out a flower from the bouquet and gives it to the counselor. He exits.)

(Lights Out)

End of Play

VERONICA BUNNY READ HER TEXT MESSAGES

An Adult Bedtime Play

Character

Veronica Bunny, mature rabbit, mother of Louie, a young adult gender-fluid rabbit

Setting

The weekly meeting of the Queer Bunny Support Group at the Beatrice Potter Center for Small Mammal Support. It's Veronica's turn to share with the group.

(Lights Rise)

VERONICA: My turn to share? I'm a little nervous... Thank you everyone for welcoming me to the Queer Bunny Support Group. This is my first time at one of your meetings, but I've hopped by the Beatrice Potter Center at least a dozen times... Always wanting to come in, but always a little bit afraid.

My name is Veronica Bunny, and I'm here because of my offspring Louie. He's a queer rabbit, gender-fluid.

(Pause)

First time I've said that out loud to a group of people. It feels comforting to say it… Comforting to know that I'm not the only parent who loves a child who doesn't… I stopped asking myself do I have a boy bunny or a girl bunny? Now I accept that I have my Louie, and a boy/girl is who he is. And by the way, he's a terrific cook. I've always found it curious that he took such an interest in food beyond survival. "Food preparation is part of becoming a civilized small-mammal society, Mom." He grows carrots himself, preserves them whole, minced, and pickled.

(VERONICA reaches into an Easter basket and takes out sample jars of treats that she distributes to members of the support group.)

I brought you some samples… Louie creates his own recipes and they're simply delicious. *Carrot Chutney* for you, dear. *Sweet and Sour Carrot Relish, Jerk Carrot Sauce* for you, Jamaican Rasta Bunnies, and *Thai Carrot Red Curry*. Enjoy and tell your friends. He has a web site now, www:LouieBunnyCooks.com.

I said I was here because of Louie.

(Pause)

Truth is, Louie is fine. I'm here for me… So that I…

I was a member of another group, The Joint Commission of Small Mammals for Social Justice. I attended their annual meeting last month, and I neglected to turn off my cell phone. Louie created some hip-hop tune to alert me to his incoming text messages. Everyone in the meeting heard it.

(Rapped to a Hip-Hop rhythm)

Here comes Louie Cotton Tail
Hopping down the bunny trail
I said hippity hop hippity hop hop hop don't stop
Peace

Then came the text: I LUV U MOM XOXO.
I automatically said out loud, "I love you back,
Louie."
As I fumbled trying to put the phone on vibrate,
Louie sent his second ring message:
I'm pink, I know it, I'm not afraid to show it... Yo, I'm
pink, I know it, I'm not afraid to show it...

Followed by another text, this time a bunny joke.
Did you hear the one about the rabbit who jumps off
bridges? He's the Easter bungee.

He's always been a funny kid.

I'm laughing hysterically, and I hear: "Something,
you want to share Veronica Bunny?" I heard this
screeching voice through a microphone in the
conference room. "Perhaps your text messages are
so important that they deserve all of our attention."
It was then that I looked up and realized that the
loud voice and all of the scornful eyes of the
membership attending the annual meeting were
looking at me. I wasn't going to text back until
after the keynote address. The conference room
hushed like there was a hunter was in the room.
"By all means," said Madame Jack Rabbit, "Share
your important text messages with all of the small
mammals at this invitation-only conference, many
of whom have traveled for miles, avoiding all sorts
of natural disasters and dangerous predators to

get here. In fact, Veronica Bunny, I'll step aside from the podium so you can interrupt a meeting that concerns our future so that you can share whatever frivolous text messages you have with our members. I'm sure the details of your manicure/pedicure appointments or bunny fur trim are far more important than how small mammals are going to cooperate and work together to insure we don't have an early extinction!"

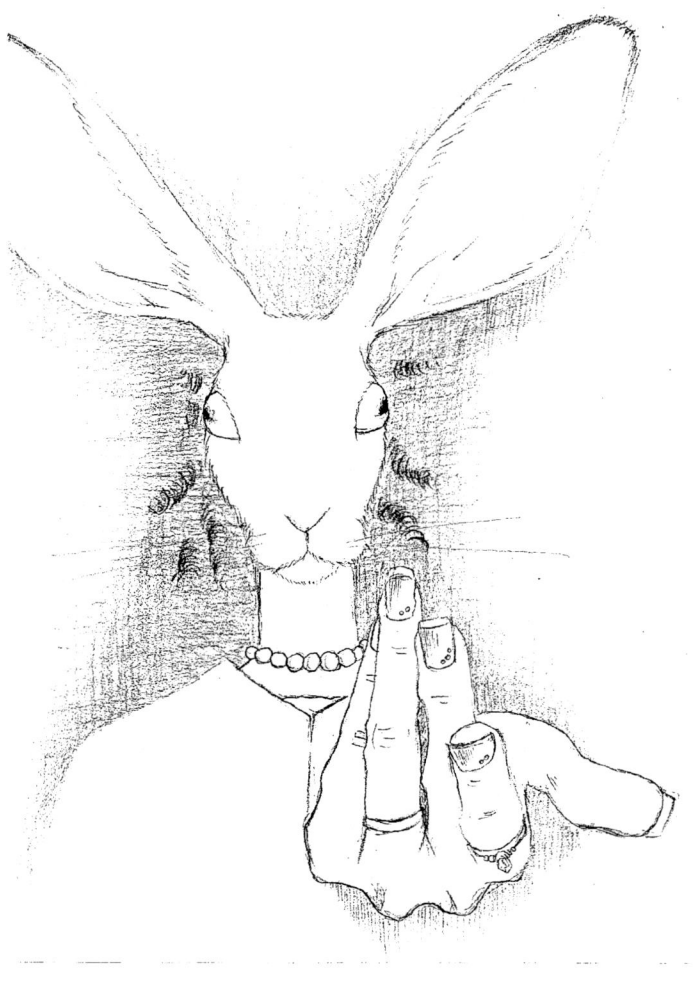

Do you know Madame Jack Rabbit? She has a
sharp tongue and a spontaneous wit. She was like
a general commanding a militia of small mammals
at attention to provide unified frowny faces at me.
Madame Jack Rabbit remained on the speaker's
platform but stepped to the side of the podium…
All of the small mammals in the room prepared for
the continued public shaming of me.

But I was smiling like I was crowned "Queen
Small Mammal for the Day" until I heard one of
the whispered comments: "That's the mother of
that queer bunny. The one that doesn't know if
he's a girl or a boy." I hopped to the front of the
conference room and stood behind the podium, a
little shaken:

"Text messages," I said, "from my son Louie. I love
you Mom. Hugs and Kisses and a Rabbit joke. Did
you ever hear the one about…

"Thank you, Veronica Bunny, for sharing" Madame
Jack Rabbit announced to the group, "We'll take
a short break now and then continue with our
planned agenda. We need to vote on the proposals
for the spring parade."

"How is Caroline?" I said to Madame Jack Rabbit.

"How my daughter Caroline is…is none of your
business," she snapped at me.

"I wanted you to know I wished her well. Louie
told me, she's had a hard time recovering from her
partner Suzette's death," I said.

"Not that it's any of your concern, but Caroline
has been confused. I'm sorry her friend died. No
rabbit should die from a bunny virus, but as far as

I'm concerned, Caroline's experimenting with girl bunnies got out of hand. Maybe I can finally get her into counseling to reverse this sickness. Bunny love is not a girl bunny who loves another girl bunny. And it's not a boy bunny who dresses like a girl."

I was frozen for a few minutes. I hopped back to my chair and picked up my Easter basket. I decided then that I was leaving. Before I got to the door, a black-footed ferret came over. "My offspring don't have black feet. All their lives they've been ridiculed. *"How can you be a black-footed ferret without black feet?"* We didn't exchange any words. We hugged.

When my kid played dress up with my clothes at home when he was four, I considered it normal. All kids like to dress up. Then when he was in kindergarten, he wanted to dress up in girl's clothes for school. He would announce each day. I'm a girl. The next day, I'm a boy.

Sometimes he wore an Easter bonnet and his boy clothes… I'm a boy girl today. What was at first my child's cuteness became my stress and anxiety, never knowing what Louie would announce each day. He was perfectly happy, but I wasn't. One day I asked him, Are you a boy, a girl, or a boy-girl today Louie? He said, I'm me. That's when I decided to home-school him… Not for him, for me… Because I was embarrassed. I loved my child. I didn't love me, the mother of the bunny who was different. I didn't want to have to be that brave. I could love him at home, but I couldn't love him in public. I was weak, and I was ashamed of me.

My text messages from Louie are priceless. I LUV U MOM XOXO. That's my social justice. My son's acceptance of me.

(Lights Out)

The End

TEMPORARY ASSOCIATIONS

Farm to Table

Characters

Judy: Female, hybrid red radish

Lenora: Female, natural red radish

Radish Handler: Male truck driver for Radish Delights

Setting

The present. Assignment and shipping garage of Radish Delights Processing Plant. Judy is seated on a shelf and waiting. Enter Lenora.

(Lights Rise)

LENORA: Hello. I'm Lenora.

JUDY: Judy.

LENORA: How are you?

 (Pause)

 This is exciting.

 (Pause)

 I guess I'm in the right place.

(Pause)

JUDY: Do you have a number?

LENORA: Sure.

(Looking in handbag.)

Somewhere. Let me see. My purse is such a mess, one big hole... I drop everything in... And I didn't think it was important... Here it is.

(Pulling out a sign that reads "387.")

JUDY: You must be from the California Appa Valley?

LENORA: Uh-huh.

JUDY: You have a surprise waiting for you.

LENORA: Excuse me?

JUDY: Radishes from Appa are so naïve.

LENORA: You don't know me.

JUDY: Never mind. You'll find out soon enough.

LENORA: Where's your top?

(Pause)

The beautiful leafy greens that should be attached to your body?

(Pause)

Mine is gorgeous, don't you think? Full California sun, rain- water conditioning, and hand-picking. I don't mind sharing my secrets. All radishes should be beautiful. Oooh, I'm sorry. Insensitive, huh? I assumed your baldness, no leafy top, was your choice... Did you have that disease that kills leaf follicles. Radipecia?

JUDY: I'm going to help you out, and then I need my quiet time.

LENORA: Okay...I was trying to be nice.

JUDY: It's very important that you listen for the Radish Handler's roll call so you can hear your number. Your number is before mine, so if you miss the roll call you'll be replaced with another radish.

LENORA: I don't understand.

JUDY: Don't they teach you California radishes anything? We're in the same crate, the three hundred batches. I'm the last radish in the box, and the crates don't leave Radish Delights without an exact count. This is a very fast-moving radish processing plant. The handlers are already going to be angry with you, so don't make waves by being late with the roll call. You want to keep your assignment.

LENORA: Angry at me? No one gets angry with me. Everyone likes me. Except, maybe...you... I'm beautiful, and I'm a very friendly radish.

JUDY: You skipped the barbershop, you radhead dimwit.

LENORA: You must be from a New York City farm, because you're bad-mannered and...

JUDY: Lenora...is it? Lenora, you shouldn't be in the assignment room until you've been shaved. When the handlers see your leafiness, they'll be upset because they'll have to send you to the barbershop before they can pack you and leave. The whole crate will have to stay open until you get back. I can't go into the crate because I'm the last radish in the three hundred series box. Our box hasn't been assigned. When it's assigned, the case has to be ready for transport, which means you've disrupted the entire operation for hundreds of radishes at Radish Delights.

LENORA: Excuse me. The barbershop...you mean the place where the radishes with the beautiful green leafy manes go in one door and come out the other door looking like you bald and unappealing.

JUDY: Yes, your majesty.

LENORA: I wasn't interested in that, so I came straight here.

JUDY: You're not allowed to do that.

LENORA: Why not?

JUDY: Every radish gets shaved so we can all fit in the box and maintain the inventory count.

LENORA: I'm in the wrong assignment place or the wrong transport place, or whatever because I'm a farm-to-table radish. People love me for my taste and beauty. They love my green leafy top and the whole Hollywood illusion of freshness and natural glamour.

JUDY: Keep believing that.

LENORA: What can I do now? How do I get out of here? Is there a back door or something?

(Lenora stands and looks around for an escape.)

JUDY: Your root is still on!

LENORA: Of course. I was pulled straight up out of the nitrogen-rich California soil.

JUDY: They have a root remover department here. Does that bright red color rub off? Can you get lighter?

LENORA: No. I'm a genuine born red.

JUDY: This just gets worse. That means you won't match the rest of us. We're all dyed hybrids. We're grown hydroponically without visible roots.

(Pause)

You, Miss. California Sunshine, have ruined the work for everyone.

LENORA: There's one thing I understand about this terrible situation. You don't want me here, and I don't want to be here.

(Pause)

Will you help me find the farm- to-table radishes?

JUDY: Give me your number.

(Lenora gives Judy her number sign.)

JUDY (Cont'd): Find some way to slick down and hide that leafy mane of yours.

LENORA: I don't have any leaf maintainer products with me.

43

JUDY: Find something in that purse if you want to get out of here.

(Lenora looks through her purse.)

LENORA: Leaf grease.

(Lenora applies the grease.)

(Sound Effect: Sound of a large truck starting)

JUDY: When you hear "387" called, jump down. You'll be on the garage floor... Run straight and fast toward the garage door.

(Enter Radish Handler)

RADISH HANDLER: "387"

(Judy takes Radish Handler's hand. He looks her over, inspecting her, picks her up, and they get in the truck. Lenora jumps simultaneously and lands on the garage floor. Radish handler drives the truck forward.)

RADISH HANDLER: Farm-to-table markets, Hollywood, California. Moving out.

(Sound Effect: Truck moving)

LENORA: Huh? (Screams)

(Lenora is crushed under truck wheels.)

(Sound Effect: Truck stops)

(Radish Handler stops the truck briefly, and then continues driving.)

(Lights Out)

End of Play

CHAKALAKA

Remembered

Characters

MELVINA: A twenty-something African American woman working as a cashier in the Chakalaka supermarket. MELVINA has two jobs. She has a waitress job during the day at a local Soul Food restaurant. Then she has her cashier job on the late shift. She is usually tired when she gets to the Chakalaka store, although she does rest between jobs.

VALERIE: A twenty-something African American woman head cashier in the Chakalaka supermarket. She is an undergraduate college student at a local public university. VALERIE lives at home and uses her meager salary from Chakalaka to supplement school expenses not covered by her scholarship.

ANNIE: An African American woman in her late thirties whose appearance makes her seem much older than her actual years. Her clothes are clean but matronly and frayed. She appears disheveled, with unkempt hair, clothes improperly buttoned and shoes with worn heels. ANNIE lives a hermitic life in her studio apartment in Harlem. She has a PhD in Italian Studies, which includes scholarly study of Italian language, literature and culture. She works at home doing Italian language translation. ANNIE rarely leaves her apartment. Chakalaka is her local neighborhood supermarket.

TY (TYRONE): The Chakalaka store security guard. He works three jobs, all as a security guard. He is usually the only male store employee in the supermarket during the late shift, so he is especially protective of the women who work in the store.

Setting

Circa 1990s. The story begins in Chakalaka, a twenty-four-hour neighborhood supermarket in Harlem. It is about 2:00 A.M. The date is July 28, the anniversary of the death of the Venetian baroque composer Antonio Lucio Vivaldi, who is believed to have died July 28, 1741. We hear a radio station playing contemporary Hip-Hop music. The music is interrupted by an automatic announcement. We see two cashiers at their registers. There are no customers. One cashier, MELVINA, is reading magazines on a magazine rack next to her register. The other cashier VALERIE, is doing "busy" cleaning work around her workstation. We see the security guard TY positioned in the front of the store giving out store circulars.

(Lights Rise)

VOICE Remember shoppers; you can get everyday values when you shop using your Chakalaka discount card.

(The Hip-Hop music resumes and fades.)

TY: Valerie, I'm gonna take my break now and get something to eat. It's pretty quiet.

(TY exits the store through the storage room door.)

MELVINA: I don't know why you bother to do all that cleaning up. Don't nobody care.

VALERIE: I just can't stand to be around mess. It's just nasty. If I have to be here all night, I might as well be in a clean space.

MELVINA: Wow…check this out.

(Melvina points out an article she is reading to Valerie.)

This says, "A famous west coast Hip-Hop artist, who wants to remain anonymous, was kidnapped by aliens and then found unconscious and naked at his music studio on 115th Street."

VALERIE: Why do you believe that trash?

MELVINA: Because it's true. They wouldn't write it unless it was true.

VALERIE: Now that's real ignorant. Just because you read it doesn't mean it's true. They're just trying to sell papers.

(Melvina looks up.)

MELVINA: Hell no! She ain't been in here for two days. I swear I thought we'd seen the last of her.

(Annie enters Chakalaka pushing a shopping cart. The shopping cart is full of store circulars, jars of coins, and clothes.)

MELVINA (Cont'd): Where's Ty?

VALERIE: He's out on break.

MELVINA: Shit.

> (Annie rolls in slowly looking around. She concentrates on the displays at the beginning of each aisle.
> The ones that say "specials.")

MELVINA: You're gonna ring her up, Valerie. I took care of her the last time. She bout to make me crazy. She never has her Chakalaka card. She always pays with coins. And she always be beggin for free stuff with those old, outdated circulars. And she stinks!

VALERIE: Alright, alright, I'll take care of her. I swear Mel, you have no patience. We're not even busy.

MELVINA: Ty ain't even here. What if she tries to start some trouble up in here?

> (Annie looks around. She takes things off the shelves, and then she puts them back. Takes items off, then puts them back. Takes items and puts them on Melvina's counter. Melvina puts the CLOSED sign on her counter.)

MELVINA: See this. It says CLOSED, Miss. Can you read it? Closed.

> (Annie looks around.)

ANNIE: You don't have any customers.

MELVINA: Closed.

VALERIE: I'll take care of you over here, Miss Annie.

MELVINA: And I hope you have your Chakalaka card. We not supposed to give the sale price without the Chakalaka card!

(Annie places several bottles of sparkling water on the counter.)

VALERIE: Find everything you need, Miss Annie? I see you like the sparkling water.

ANNIE: You got any more?

VALERIE: You have all of the eight-ounce bottles we have. Would you like four-ounce?

ANNIE: Only eight-ounce. It was eight-ounce. Check in the back.

MELVINA: She's crazy. She buys all the sparkling water in glass bottles. She always makes Ty go in the back to see if there are unopened cases. Then she buys all of them. I saw her open up all of the bottles outside the store then empty them right in the street. What kind of person buys bottles of water then empties the water in the street? A crazy person, that's who.

VALERIE: Miss Annie, I'm sure you have all of the eight-ounce bottles in the store. We can't check in the back. We have to stay in the front of the store.

ANNIE: I'll be back tomorrow. Don't sell those bottles to nobody, nobody else, you hear me!

MELVINA: Oh, Lord…I knew it…she's gonna go crazy up in here. How we posed to be professional when we got low-lifes coming in the store?

VALERIE: Stop it, Mel. I'm gonna try to keep her calm. I learned about this in my psych class.

(Annie empties some coins and begins to count them slowly.)

ANNIE: Twenty-five, fifty, seventy-five, one dollar…

VALERIE: Here let me help you. You finish shopping.

MELVINA: I'm not feelin good about this, Valerie. Hurry up. Get her outta here. Ty is takin a long time to get back.

VALERIE: Is there something else you need, Miss Annie?

ANNIE: I need detergent. What do you have on special?

(Annie takes the circulars out of her shopping cart.)

MELVINA: I told you. She's got those old circulars. Those circulars are too old.

(Valerie interrupts her as she takes piles of old circulars out of her shopping cart.)

VALERIE: It's O.K. I have the new circular right here. Let's see what we have on sale.

MELVINA: Ask her; ask her if she has her Chakalaka card. She don't have it. I know she don't have it.

ANNIE: I don't have my store card.

VALERIE: Don't worry. You can use mine.

(Valerie swipes her store card on the scanner.)

O.K. We have Tide.

ANNIE: Tried it.

VALERIE: Tide with bleach.

ANNIE: Too expensive.

VALERIE: Tide Ultra.

ANNIE: That ultra is hype. You still have to use a lot.

VALERIE: Arm & Hammer.

ANNIE: Too natural.

VALERIE: Arm & Hammer for heavy duty loads.

ANNIE: Not natural enough.

VALERIE: We have the store brand---Chakalaka.

(Annie looks at Valerie.)

ANNIE: No!

(Annie looks at Melvina, then walks aggressively toward her.)

NO! NO! NO!

(Annie roams to the front of the store as she continues
to talk. While Annie recollects her experience the faded
Hip-Hop music is replaced by Antonio Vivaldi's concerto
"L'estate,"
The Four Seasons- Summer Movement 3: Presto, softly.
The music resonates throughout the supermarket.
Lights indicate time and place change to the past.)

ANNIE: I have to get the stain out. I have to get the
stain out. Faccia Bella...he called me Faccia Bella. It
means beautiful face. They are lovely words. They
are words of endearment, words of caring, words

you use when you treasure someone. But he made those beautiful words dirty.

MELVINA: I'm scared, Valerie. What's she talking about?

(Annie speaks with two different male-like voices in addition to her own voice.
As she speaks we hear the tension and the frenzy of the Vivaldi concerto.)

ANNIE (as JOEY): What's that hoe doing in the neighborhood?

ANNIE (as ANTHONY): I don't know, but she needs to get her Black ass to Bed Sty, Fort Green, or wherever those jiggaboos come from.

ANNIE (as JOEY): Hey Anthony, why don't we taste some Black meat? You know I hear they're like animals especially if you take it from the back. You know those fat asses take a lot of punch.

ANNIE (as ANTHONY): Are you sick? Their cunts stink and they have all kinds of diseases! Don't you know, that's why we have AIDS? It's a jiggaboos disease. No, I say let's teach the bitch a lesson. Yo--- isn't that what you people say? Yo!

(ANNIE laughs as ANTHONY and JOEY.)

ANNIE (as ANTHONY): Faccia Bella. I just want to talk to you.

(Valerie and Melvina are mystically joined into Annie's narration of her story.
The music of the Vivaldi's concerto builds as the assailants proceed with their mission to teach Annie a lesson.

(The separation of present day and past is blurred. Annie, Valerie and Melvina enact the assault.)

VALERIE: I kept walking. I tried not to hear them.

MELVINA: I just needed to get to the train.

VALERIE: The bus wasn't running.

MELVINA: I just needed to get to the train.

ANNIE (as ANTHONY): Didn't you hear me? I'm trying to be nice. Faccia Bella, I just want to talk to you.

VALERIE: They ran ahead of me.

ANNIE (as JOEY): What are you doing here?

MELVINA: They blocked me from moving.

ANNIE (as ANTHONY): Only whores and hookers are out this time of night. So which are you?

(The beauty of the concerto becomes distorted.
Vivaldi accelerando, forte.)

ANNIE: Vi prego, lasciatemi in pace. Voglio andare al treno. Sto andando a casa.[1]

(ANNIE laughs as ANTHONY and JOEY)

ANNIE (as JOEY): Anthony, she speaks the ling better than us.

ANNIE (as ANTHONY): Shut up, bitch. Shut up. Italian is a white people's language.

VALERIE: I couldn't stop talking.

ANNIE: Vi prego, non cerco guai.

MELVINA: Please, I don't want any trouble.

ANNIE: Sto solo cercando di andare a casa.

VALERIE: I'm just trying to get home.

ANNIE: Stavo studiando per un esame d'italiano con un amico.

MELVINA: I was here just studying for an Italian exam with a friend.

ANNIE (as ANTHONY): You're lying.

ANNIE: He slapped me.

ANNIE (as ANTHONY): Nobody in this neighborhood is a friend with your kind. I say you're a hoe.

ANNIE: Joey says, "Not here, Ant. Take her under the bridge. Do her there."

ANNIE (as ANTHONY: Shut up Joey. I told you their cunts are full of diseases. I'm gonna teach this bitch a lesson.

(Melvina and Valerie are the chorus of Annie's opera of despair and suffering.)

MELVINA: He knocked me down.

VALERIE: One pulled me while the other one looked out.

ANNIE (as ANTHONY): What you gotta do is make the lesson count. Make sure these jiggaboos don't forget.

(Valeria and Melvina move in unison as the distorted concerto underscores Annie's recall of the assault.)

VALERIE & MELVINA: *We were under the bridge.*
    There was sand.
    There was the beach.
    There were garbage cans.

(Vivaldi, extra forte. Annie falls to the floor of the supermarket.)

ANNIE: He ripped my panties then he pushed an empty water bottle inside me up the back…an eight ounce sparkling water bottle. Prego, prego, I don't want to die. Don't hurt me!

VALERIE & MELVINA: *He kept pushing.*

ANNIE: *I kept bleeding.*

VALERIE & MELVINA: *He kept pushing.*

ANNIE: *I kept bleeding.*

(Pause)

ANNIE: He threw some coins on me while I laid in the sand. That should be enough for a jiggaboo hoe.

(Vivaldi staccato)

ANNIE (as ANTHONY): Ciao Bella.

ANNIE (as JOEY): Ciao Bella.

ANNIE, MELVINA & VALERIE: The blood was all over my dress, my white dress.

(Vivaldi staccato)

ANNIE: I had to get on the train with that bloodstained white dress. It took two hours from

Brooklyn to Harlem on the train. I couldn't sit. There was still broken glass in my... I had to stand dripping blood on the train. Then I had to walk home from the train to my house with those bloodstains on my white dress, with the blood dripping.

ANNIE: *Everybody saw the blood.*

ANNIE, MELVINA & VALERIE*: Everybody on the train saw the blood.*
Everybody in the street saw the blood.
Nobody said anything.

ANNIE: *Nobody helped me.*

(Vivaldi soft to fade)

ANNIE: When I got home I took the dress off, and I put it in the sink to soak. I couldn't get the blood out.

MELVINA & VALERIE: I couldn't get the blood out.

ANNIE: I couldn't get the blood out.

(Valerie and Melvina exit Annie's narration of her assault. Present day supermarket lighting.
Annie pulls an old soiled white dress out of her shopping cart and hands it to Valerie.)

ANNIE (Cont'd): I need a different detergent. I need a detergent that works. I have to get the blood out.

(Valerie takes the soiled dress and lays it on the counter. She reaches into her pocketbook under the counter.)

VALERIE: I can help you. I keep this in my pocketbook because I'm always getting spills on my clothes. It's really good. It even works on old stains. Let me try it on your dress.

(Valerie uses a stain remover pen rubbing back and forth on the stain.)

VALERIE (Cont'd): When it dries, it will look even better. But it's working. See, the stain is getting lighter. Maybe all of it won't come out, but most of it will.

(Valerie gently folds the dress in a neat square and hands the dress to Annie.)

VALERIE (Cont'd): Here's your dress back, Miss Annie.

(Annie looks at the dress.)

ANNIE: You got it out. You got the bloodstain out.

VALERIE: Most of it is gone.

(Annie looks at Valerie.)

ANNIE: (Annie expresses herself with words and gestures) Posso gettario via.[2]

(She starts to walk away. She leaves the shopping cart with the circulars.)

MELVINA: You have to take that with you. You can't leave that shopping cart with all that trash up in here.

VALERIE: Stop it, Mel! Leave her alone.

(Annie walks towards Valerie, and she stands in front of her at an intimate distance.)

ANNIE: A volte non possiamo fare le cose da soli. Una mano amica, una mano gentile e'necessaria.

Grazie. Grazie.[3]
Ciao

MELVINA: What is she saying?

VALERIE: I think she's speaking Italian.

MELVINA: Black people speak Italian?

VALERIE: Mel, don't be ridiculous.

(Annie leaves the store.)

Thank you doesn't have a language.

(TY enters Chakalaka from the storage room.)

TY: Anybody want some food? I picked up some eats on my break.

(Melvina and Valerie are quiet, staring at the shopping cart.)

TY: Anything happen while I was gone?

MELVINA: Yeah, that...

VALERIE: Mel.

MELVINA: Nothin.

(TY points to the shopping cart.)

TY: Where did that come from? Looks like that shopping cart crazy Annie always pushes around.

VALERIE: She was here. But she won't be back. You can put that cart in the back with the trash.

TY: But...

MELVINA: Forget about it, Ty.

(Ty removes the cart and begins to take it to the back of
the store. Music from the radio begins to play.
The automatic announcement is heard over the loud
speaker.)

VOICE: You'll always find what you need at your local
Chakalaka store. If you don't see it, just ask for help
from one of our pleasant sales associates.

(Melvina begins to read the tabloids again. Valerie starts
cleaning up her counter with a spray cleaner and a rag.)

MELVINA: Look at this one. It says the ghost of Elvis
was seen at the Apollo on...

VALERIE: Mel!

(Fade to Black)

(As the lights fade to black, the contemporary Hip-Hop music
remixed with Vivaldi is heard.)

(Lights Out)

End of Play

Footnotes

1 Please, leave me alone. I just want to get to the train. I'm going home.

2 Throw it away.

3 Sometimes we can't do things alone. A helping hand, a kind hand is needed. Thank you. Thank you.

Acknowledgment

Alice Ghellini assisted with the Italian language translation.

THE CHOSEN FRUIT

All Hail the Republic

Characters

Pablo Peel: unripe yellow banana peel

Babette Banana: banana fruit

Setting

The present.

A banana grove in Panama on a bright sunny day. Pablo and Babette wait to ripen.

(Lights Rise)

BABETTE: Pablo?

PABLO: Hung?

BABETTE: Are you okay?

PABLO: Yes...okay...I was just...

BABETTE: You were just dreaming.

PABLO: No...not un sueno...all my dreams end the same way, with an assassin holding a machete to our stem.

BABETTE: You shouldn't call the farm workers assassins. Besides, that's our reality. Should happen soon, don't you think...the harvest? What color are you now?

(Pause)

You're here with me, but you seem so far away.

PABLO: I was having an out-of-peel experience.

(Pause)

I was here, but I felt like I was a part of a larger reality. We were together at the top of the banana tree. I felt the sun on my peel, the breeze coming from the Canal de Panama. The bunches of bananas from the other trees were here, but there was no separation between you and me or any other banana. I felt a oneness. I was relaxed...at peace...

BABETTE: Maybe you were dreaming of banana pudding.

PABLO: It was something more... I've never felt this way.

BABETTE: Pablo, you are always trying to make something bigger than it is. We are a banana and a banana peel, nothing more, nothing less.

PABLO: Babette, I believe there is more. My experience confirms it. We have something to live for.

BABETTE: Yes, we live to be eaten.

PABLO: I think there is an afterlife.

BABETTE: You mean something that happens after we're harvested, besides being eaten?

PABLO: Yes, something more.

BABETTE: Oh...I understand... You mean the Banana Republic!

PABLO: What's that?

BABETTE: I think it must be a special place Shaquita will send us after we're harvested. I heard some bananas saying that the farm workers wore shirts with labels that said,

"Banana Republic."

PABLO: That's a myth, just like Shaquita is a myth.

BABETTE: You don't believe in Shaquita?

PABLO: "Shaquita," the great giver of life and death to bananas, is only folklore.

BABETTE: You mustn't say such things. It's blasphemy. The other bananas could hear you.

PABLO: The "Shaquita" story was created by the growers to keep bananas enslaved.

BABETTE: I believe in Shaquita. It's only because of Shaquita that we are "The Chosen Fruit."

PABLO: All fruit is equal.

BABETTE: Perhaps... But bananas are special. And being the Chosen Fruit, we have responsibilities.

(Pause)

I've seen Shaquita in my banana mind. She wears a long flowing blue skirt with ruffles. She has a midriff top that exposes her belly button, and she's curvy.

PABLO: I can't believe you've blindly accepted the stories.

BABETTE: And then there's her hat. She carries a very large straw basket on her head filled with bananas.

PABLO: And what happened to the other fruit?

BABETTE: The creation story tells us that Shaquita was in a great plantation with many kinds of fruit. Fruit growing on bushes and in greenhouses. She looked around and saw low-hanging fruit and fruit atop trees and said, *Behold... It shall be that the bananas shall be The Chosen Fruit, for it is only the banana that rises above all others growing in the tallest plant.*

PABLO: Banana grove myth... That's all...

BABETTE: Then what about the prayer?

PABLO: What prayer?

BABETTE: (Hums the Shaquita Banana jingle)

And from a few yellow bananas...
      many bananas were created...

Go forth and multiply in every tropical nation. You shall grow in bunches. You shall grow in colors...yellow, green, pink. I tell you, bananas, for it is now as the chosen fruit that you will be first. The first fruit to nourish babies after mother's milk, and the first fruit for runners after a marathon.

PABLO: Did you ever ask yourself what happens to other fruit?

BABETTE: It's not our concern. There are bananas, and them. And their salvation is not our concern.

PABLO: You have an enslaved banana mind.

BABETTE: What do you mean, enslaved?

PABLO: You've accepted the myth of Shaquita, and the myth has enslaved you without you realizing it. You've given your life to the myth of Shaquita instead of cherishing your own existence.

BABETTE: Loco! Again… You try to make something "big" out of nothing. Shaquita takes care of us. We don't have any worries.

PABLO: I want to finish telling you my nightmare. The one you pointed out is our reality.

(Pause)

The banana man will come. He'll cut down the bunches of bananas and then load us all into trucks. We'll be placed on ships waiting at the docks in the Panama Canal. Thousands of bananas piled on top of each other in cargo hulls. We won't be able to move.

BABETTE: We don't move much now.

PABLO: You'll understand freedom when it's taken away.

BABETTE: Where will they take us?

PABLO: Probably Miami.

BABETTE: Could be nice?

PABLO: Doesn't anything I say disturb you?

BABETTE: Shaquita loves us.

PABLO: Shaquita is a myth for the growers. Wake up. We're property.
We shouldn't belong to anyone.

BABETTE: Don't tell me anymore. Again… You're trying to make something big that isn't. It doesn't matter.

PABLO: It does matter. We don't have to go.

BABETTE: We do have to go. All bananas leave the plantation when it's time.

PABLO: I haven't ripened.

BABETTE: I'm ripe. You're ripe. You're a beautiful color green.

PABLO: I should be yellow.

BABETTE: No… "guineo verde." We're a green banana.

PABLO: Look around you. We're an unripened yellow banana. Look at the rest of the bunch. Everyone is yellow.

BABETTE: You're just a little late. Too much sun or not enough sun…don't worry Shaquita will take care of us.

PABLO: We aren't platanos! Do you think your Shaquita will treat us like a cooking banana, like a vegetable instead of a fruit because my peel is green?

BABETTE: Then fix this. Make us a green cooking banana.

PABLO: We can't become something we're not.

BABETTE: (She begins humming the Shaquita banana jingle.)

PABLO: Do you think your prayers to Shaquita will change this?

(Pause)

Do you know what happens to yellow bananas that don't turn green fast enough?

BABETTE: (She hums the jingle louder and stronger.)

PABLO: They get sent to the gas chamber.

BABETTE: Noooooooooooooooo.

PABLO: Listen to me...

BABETTE: Noooooooooooooooo.

PABLO: We won't be left to ripen on the tree. We'll be sent to the gas greenhouse and sprayed with ethylene gas to force ripening.

BABETTE: I don't believe you. Shaquita loves us. We're The Chosen Fruit.

PABLO: We're property of the growers.

(Pause)

BABETTE: If we're going to the gas greenhouse, it must be for our own good.

PABLO: Babette, if I know anything about you, it's that you always wanted to be tree-ripened.

BABETTE: Yes…I never considered anything else. I thought staying in the grove until I was ready to be eaten was natural.

PABLO: That can't happen now.

BABETTE: I want to be eaten by a marathon runner!

PABLO: Our destiny is one in the same. If I don't ripen, you'll never be eaten.

(Pause)

There's a way out. I think that's what my out-of-peel experience was telling me. I need to break the invisible chains of my enslavement to the growers and be free to choose my own destiny. We'll have to do it together.

BABETTE: What choices? I don't see any choices.

PABLO: We can rot.

BABETTE: What is that?

PABLO: We can fall to the ground. We'll be left to decay. We'll become fertilizer for the earth beneath us.

(Pause)

Something like pudding…only helping plants grow.

BABETTE: All plants?

PABLO: All plants. In the world of decay, there's no Chosen Fruit. We exist, we live, and we rot.

BABETTE: I don't want to hear any more of your crazy talk. Maybe we'll have to go to the gas chamber…because of you… You've been in the sun too long. The heat is making you crazy. I believe in Shaquita. I believe in Shaquita. I believe in Shaquita. We are the Chosen Fruit. We are The Chosen Fruit. We are The Chosen Fruit…

PABLO: We have to do this together. You have all the weight in our relationship. Pull as hard as you can when you feel the cut of the machete so we can separate from the bunch and fall. We won't be missed. We'll be left on the ground.

BABETTE: You confuse me. I need simple. I don't want to think about these crazy things. You stay…I want to go with the bunch.

PABLO: You know I can't stay without you. I can't peel myself away from you.

BABETTE: You're asking me to do something I know nothing about. To choose the unknown.

What if you're wrong about decay?

(Pause)

PABLO: What if you're right about Banana Republic?

(Lights Out)
End of Play

LINEA NEGRA

A Fine Line

Characters

Roberta: Guardian of the Blackness of Linea Negra
lovely, sexy Latina, forty- to fifty-something

Graciella: Guardian of the Length of Linea Negra
lovely, sexy Latina, thirty-something

Setting

The top of the nine-month pregnant belly of Dianna
Sanchez. Roberta and Graciella have lawn chairs on
opposite sides in the middle of the Linea Negra, a dark
black line that extends in the middle of the body from
the height of Dianna's breasts to her belly button. Roberta is seated, playing Baby Name Scrabble. Graciella is
dancing various fast paced Latin dances up, down, and
around the line (Merengue, Salsa, and Bachata).

(Lights Rise)

ROBERTA: (Stops reading and looks over at Linea Negra)
Line looks good today, Graciella.

GRACIELLA: Absolutely, perfectamente negra. Perfect
color black.. Perfect color black. ¡Baila conmigo!

ROBERTA: I used the Blackness Meter yesterday, but I suppose it wouldn't hurt to take measurements today. You should really play Baby Name Scrabble with me sometime instead of shaking the baby up with all of your dancing.

GRACIELLA: She does her own shaky moving inside her Mami. This chica loves.

(Speaking to the belly)

Right, mi amor?

ROBERTA: Graciella, do you remember where I put the Blackness Meter?

GRACIELLA: Check under your chair, Roberta. Isn't that where you usually keep it?

ROBERTA: It's not under my chair.

(Pause)

If you're going to dance Salsa, please dance on the two-count!

(Pause)

What's a four-letter girl's name that has /g/ for the third letter and /a/ for the last letter?

(Pause)

ROBERTA: Conga.

GRACIELLA: Conga? For a girl's name? Dianna isn't going to name her daughter Conga.

That's why Baby Name Scrabble is so ridiculous. Dianna and Arturo can name the baby any name they choose.

ROBERTA: Conga is sorta cute, almost sounds like "Congo." That's it. The baby could be named after the country. I'll send a message to Lucinda the voice filer to whisper the name Congo into Dianna's left ear; then she will believe she thought of the name herself and tell Arturo.

GRACIELLA: I wonder why the ancestors sent that name to us through the Scrabble game? Why don't you check the family tree book and see if there were any women in the family named Conga?

(Graciella throws the Blackness Meter under Roberta's chair while Roberta gets the family history book.)

GRACIELLA: Perhaps you're right. Conga could be a beautiful name for a baby girl.

ROBERTA: You had my Blackness Meter all this time.

(Pause)

I'm in charge of determining the intensity of the blackness.

GRACIELLA: How did measuring the blackness of the line get to be exclusively your job?

ROBERTA: It's always been my job, and measuring the length of the line has always been your job.

GRACIELLA: Breasts to the belly button. And if I want to measure the line with dance steps, then it's my business.

(Pause)

You know I can do your job just as well as you do too, Roberta.

ROBERTA: Not open for debate. I'm not interested in changing jobs.

(Roberta uses the Blackness Meter.)

ROBERTA (Cont'd): Excellent. 9.98. Two-points higher than yesterday. She's going to deliver this baby at any time.

GRACIELLA: The Linea Negra will need to move below the belly button first.

ROBERTA: Not true for Dianna. It's simply genetic. The women in her family line have had lines that stop precisely at the top of the belly button.

GRACIELLA: Not true. The Sanchez women have always had exceptionally long lines. Look in the book.

(Roberta looks and locates the section in the book.)

ROBERTA: The earliest record here refers to her ancestors during the Spanish Inquisition.

GRACIELLA: That was a terrible, sad time. Any woman with a Linea Negra was declared a witch and crucified. We couldn't protect them.

ROBERTA: There was no way to tell the length of Consuelo Sanchez's Linea Negra. The records just indicate her arrest during pregnancy when the line appeared.

GRACIELLA: Look during the reign of Queen Isabella. The pope decided the line was a blessing from God and not the mark of the devil.

ROBERTA: Luciana Sanchez, one of Christopher Columbus's lovers sailed with him to the Americas on the *Pinta* because he believed the line would bring good luck.

GRACIELLA: It didn't bring good luck to the Taino Indians he slaughtered.

ROBERTA: No mention of the length of the line.

(Pause)

No way to resolve this. We have to watch for the pulsating of the line. Then we'll know if Dianna is in labor. But you probably have the baby all confused with your dancing. You're going to convince the baby to come early.

GRACIELLA: She's enough weeks to be born now. We can't wait for pulsations. We have to plan. Dianna wants to get back to her modeling work. The line doesn't need to read ten shades of blackness for her to deliver. She's close enough.

ROBERTA: Nothing to plan. This baby is going to come when she's ready. And I've been talking to her about waiting as long as possible. Be safe and comfortable inside her Mama as long as possible. She'll face the challenges of living as a girl in a male-dominated world soon enough.

GRACIELLA: So that's what you were doing at Dianna's belly button yesterday! Talking foolishness to the baby behind my back. You think her life is going to be full of suffering like her Tia Consuelo? Ridiculous.

ROBERTA: No, I'm just saying women are still not free. Men still control the woman's body.

GRACIELLA: Don't be political. Dianna can do anything she wants with her body, and she will. She's going to start with the line. The line is too black, and makeup won't hide it enough for runway bikini modeling.

ROBERTA: There was a time when women, even those who were persecuted, were proud of their Linea Negra if they were among the few to have one. A sign of femininity and fertility. I shouldn't have to tell you this--you're a female guardian.

GRACIELLA: Blah Blah. It's a new day. She's already talked to her cosmetic advisor about options: bleaching, peels, laser, and skin grafts. We're flying to Argentina right after the baby is born to get work done.

ROBERTA: A butcher in Argentina?

GRACIELLA: She'll take care of everything in one trip. Breasts, butt, abs, skin fillers, and of course the line.

ROBERTA: You're talking about the line as if it were a stretch mark or a pimple. Linea Negra binds the woman to the baby and the baby to the mother in a way that neither can reject because it's in their genetic soul. Linea is ancestral.

GRACIELLA: I'm talking about survival.

ROBERTA: And how would that happen if the line is removed?

GRACIELLA: We'll leave a little pigment for her to get removed. She'll think the line is all gone. We'll hide the line under the top layer of the skin and sit inside her belly button until she's asleep. As she sleeps, we'll take the line out. When Dianna touches the line, the bond with the ancestors and with the baby will continue to be renewed. And when I talked to Bella Belly Button, she assured me that she has no problem with us moving in.

ROBERTA: We're not hiding the line.

GRACIELLA: We're doing it.

ROBERTA: Move away from the line, Graciella.

(Graciella rolls up the line, and an aggressive fight occurs with Roberta and Graciella attempting to get the line from the other. The fight ends with the line wrapped up under Dianna's breasts.)

(Sound Effect: Contractions)

(Physical Effect: The torso moves up and down)

GRACIELLA: Look what you've done. The whole belly is contracting.

(Roberta and Graciella fall down and roll over and over until the contractions come to a gradual stop.)

ROBERTA: False contractions.

GRACIELLA: Her husband hates the line. He told her it's unattractive and that he hopes it fades after the delivery.

ROBERTA: She wants to look good for her man.

GRACIELLA: She wants to look good for herself and not interrupt her career. She's free to do what she wants with her body. What Arturo cares about her body isn't the main issue. But look at you! No interest in Dianna having control over her own body. You want her to have a body that's pleasing to Arturo.

ROBERTA: It's the way it is. If she doesn't keep a body to please Arturo, he'll find a woman that will.

GRACIELLA: Yes, the way it is. Male guardianship and control over the female body in the earth world. Female guardianship on the metaphysical. One day... It will change...

ROBERTA: Maybe in Conga's lifetime.

(Pause)

ROBERTA (Cont'd): Let's pack up. Let's roll the line down from the breasts. Some of the line is tangled under the right breast. I'll meet you up there. The next contractions might be real.

(Graciella goes to the top of the line under the right breast.)

(Pause)

Good thing her belly button is an innie.

GRACIELLA: I need you to come up here, Roberta.

ROBERTA: I will. Let me fold up the chairs first. And I'm missing some letters for the Scra...

GRACIELLA: (Screams) Importante!

(Roberta goes to the area under the right breast.)

(Pause)

ROBERTA: What's so impor...

GRACIELLA: Do you feel it?

(Roberta feels the area around the breast.)

ROBERTA: Lumps...

(They hold each other in loving embrace.)

GRACIELLA: Madre de Dios.

(Lights Out)

End of Play

A GIRL & HER BIRD

Flying Lovers

Characters

Audrey Spelling: The Girl

Blossom: Super-Talker Hybrid Love Bird

Donovan Wallinger III: Bird Lover, entrepreneur

Jasmin Yasmin Littlejohn: Investigative reporter for
Bird View Magazine

Julius: Singing Pigeon

Setting

Daytime—Birdieville

Interior: Minimalist, dull apartment with a window facing a city street and adjacent park. There's a desk and chair and a fancy birdcage on a stand. There's a vanity, mirrors, perch, and bird piano (keyboard) inside the cage. Audrey is seated at the desk working with documents and books. Blossom is inside the cage playing her keyboard. She plays and sings a very tragic "lonely heart" song.

Exterior: Park bench next to a sidewalk and grassy

common filled with pigeons feasting on breadcrumbs. Donovan Wallington III is throwing breadcrumbs to the pigeons. Julius sits on the bench next to Donovan while occasionally corralling the pigeons into the feeding zone and then flies off.

(Lights Rise)

JASMIN YASMIN LITTLEJOHN: Hello bird lovers. This is Jasmin Yasmin Littlejohn, your sexy, and very intelligent roaming investigative reporter person with a bird's eye view (wink) for *Bird View Magazine* reporting to you live from Sparrow Lane in Birdieville. I'm outside Audrey Spelling's apartment. When we last saw Audrey, she had just broken up with her boyfriend Larry. An anonymous tip from a little birdie

(Sound Effect: Tweet Tweet)

JASMIN YASMIN LITTLEJOHN (Cont'd): has led us to suspect that Audrey is the perpetrator of bird abuse or worse. Let's look inside with our panoramic camera.

(She aims the cameras at Audrey's apartment.)

BLOSSOM: (Singing while crying)

AUDREY: (Throwing an object at the cage) Be quiet, I'm working.

BLOSSOM: Audrey, you broke my gate.

AUDREY: Doesn't matter. Not for the "bird princess." You're not moving out... Unfortunately. You've got it too good here... A better life than I have.

BLOSSOM: I'm doing what a super-talker hybrid lovebird is supposed to do--speak incessantly and sing about love.

AUDREY: Play your bird piano and shut your beak.

(Blossom hums as she plays.)

AUDREY: Blossom, you're getting on my last nerve.

BLOSSOM: I'm lonely, Audrey. I'm a lovebird with no one to love. What's a girl bird supposed to do? I'm so sad.

AUDREY: Sing a happy love song.

BLOSSOM: I can't! You played the same sad song thousands of times after you broke up with Larry. I can't get that sad song out of my birdbrain. Made me temporarily cuckoo. Why did you have to break up with him? He was a nice guy.

AUDREY: I should explain the reason to you? You're my pet mate bird, not my analyst.

BLOSSOM: You tell me about everything else-- your shopping list, your stingy second cousin Alice, your boss's toupee that looks like a dirty mop.

AUDREY: You eavesdrop when I'm talking aloud. I'm not talking to you.

BLOSSOM: We live together. I can't turn your mouth off, and you can't turn off mine... Well, my beak... Same thing, more or less.

AUDREY: Ne'er do well.

BLOSSOM: Near the well?

AUDREY: A "ne'er do well." Keeping a low-paying job, no ambition to go further, always short on cash, paycheck to paycheck living. Larry could never earn more money than me.

BLOSSOM: Larry adored you.

AUDREY: I need a better apartment, a better car, better everything, and it's not going to be with my checkbook alone.

BLOSSOM: I would choose a boy bird just for love, not money.

AUDREY: That's because you don't pay for anything, Blossom. Custom-decorated cage, gold perch, bird piano, and gourmet food delivery daily...

BLOSSOM: But you didn't buy my boyfriend. You left him in the pet store. We loved each other. Mr. Wong offered you a deal on two birds.

AUDREY: That other bird was old, sickly, and had no pedigree.

BLOSSOM: I would have cared for him until death did we part. When you love someone, you accept their shortcomings.

AUDREY: Wong said he wouldn't last a month.

BLOSSOM: Tyrone's love would have lived with me long after his death. We didn't get a chance to choose our own love song. Now all I can do is sing your sad sad love songs from your failed relationships. You can't keep a lover, so you don't want me to have one. Female jealousy...

AUDREY: (Covering the cage)
    I've had enough of you.

BLOSSOM: Take it off... I'm claustrophobic... I can't breathe... I can't see...

(Bird screams)

AUDREY: (Removing the cage cover)
    Keep your ~~mouth~~ beak shut, Blossom.

BLOSSOM: Sit me next to the window please. I need air. I need sunlight. I might pass out.

AUDREY: (Moving the cage to the open window)
    A Super-Talker Love Bird should be singing some soothing love songs or just sitting pretty, giving me a diversion when I'm not working. You're not doing either. I believe I can say with full confidence that, "I HATE YOU!"

BLOSSOM: So much better now.

(Pause)

That was immature of you. Eventually I'll forgive you for that because you're grieving. Why can't you understand my grief?

AUDREY: Your warrantee has expired, the animal shelter doesn't accept birds, and I don't have the patience for Craig's List. You've made my life miserable.

BLOSSOM: You've made your own life miserable. My emotions are simply reflecting your sadness, Audrey.

AUDREY: (packing books and papers)
Can't work in my own apartment.

BLOSSOM: Our apartment, people mate. And bring home some bird sun block, please.

(Audrey exits through the apartment door.)

JASMIN YASMIN LITTLEJOHN (Cont'd): Tragic. Worse than I could have imagined. Here are some of the twitter tweets just coming in:

Sophie from Boston says: "Sunblock is overrated. Birds need vitamin D."

Terrance from Al's Pet Store on 5th says: "I agree with Audrey, Blossom is greedy and spoiled. Audrey needs to get a new bird. I'm available. Call Al's Bird Paradise 646…"

Sorry Terrance, no advertisements unless you're a sponsor.

Fans, keep those birdie twitter tweets coming!

(She moves back to street level and hides behind a bush in the park.
She aims the camera at Julius and Donovan.)

JASMIN YASMIN LITTLEJOHN (Cont'd): We're hidden behind this bush in Sparrow Lane Park to get a bird's eye view (wink) of the notorious Donovan Wallinger III and his right hand pigeon Julius. Our source,

(Sound Effect: Tweet Tweet)

JASMIN YASMIN LITTLEJOHN (Cont'd): who shall remain anonymous, revealed that this is the site of some negotiation for the...

(Julius enters, flying to the bench.)

JASMIN YASMIN LITTLEJOHN (Cont'd): I'm going silent... The camera is rolling... Let's find out what's going down or, maybe, going up?

DONOVAN WALLINGER III: Julius, at the end of this year I want the business to be completely legitimate. I'm getting out.

JULIUS: Boss, our cash and bread crumbs have never been better.

DONOVAN WALLINGER III: I'm bleeding, Julius. I'm hustling 24/7 and losing my soul.

JULIUS: Maybe you need a partner. Reduce some of your stress.

(Pause)

Make me your partner, boss.

DONOVAN WALLINGER III: Not gonna happen, Julius.

JULIUS: No human or fowl has been more loyal to you than me. I've been your right-hand bird since you took over the business from your father, may he rest in peace.

DONOVAN WALLINGER III: Your loyalty has nothing to do with it.

JULIUS: Who recruited that flock of pigeons from the east side to take over our Long Island routes?

DONOVAN WALLINGER III: You did, but that's not the point.

JULIUS: Who negotiated the flying routes through Central Park with the other bird families?

DONOVAN WALLINGER III: Enough, Julius.

JULIUS: This is not the time to get out of the Carrier Pigeon business. We're about to go international. The Canada geese are waiting for…

DONOVAN WALLINGER III: I don't want this life anymore. My father never wanted this for me. But he died, the money was good, and I got sucked in so deep that I trapped myself.

JULIUS: Sell me the business.

DONOVAN WALLINGER III: Forget about it, Julius.

JULIUS: I can take on more responsibilities, and I could use a bigger cut of the dough.

DONOVAN WALLINGER III: You're not a man, Julius.

JULIUS: Yo, Boss… Let's not get personal. I'm a male.

DONOVAN WALLINGER III: Whatcha gonna do, Julius, fly into the Balduci Brothers headquarters and convince them to send their freight with carrier pigeons instead of trucks?

JULIUS: I'll make them an offer they can't refuse.

DONOVAN WALLINGER III: Admit it, Julius. You're looking for an opportunity to go public with your music, but you don't see that happening because...

JULIUS: Don't go there, boss...

DONOVAN WALLINGER III: Because you're a pigeon. And no one accepts pigeons in the music industry.

JULIUS: Sure... Sure... My little-bitty pigeon heart wants to forget all this and croon.

(He sings a powerful "old school"-like tune.)

DONOVAN WALLINGER III: I know you Julius. We've been working together a long time. I can see what makes you happy.

JULIUS: What do you really want, boss?

DONOVAN WALLINGER III: I'm sick of these bread crumbs, scraps of other people's baking...

JULIUS: Tell me, boss...

DONOVAN WALLINGER III: I want to bake my own bread. I'm sick of breadcrumbs from day-old bread with gluten filled flour and preservatives. I can do better than this.

(Pulling a journal out of his pocket)

This is where I write down my dreams Julius--my bread recipes.

JULIUS: I had no idea, boss.

DONOVAN WALLINGER III: I'd have our ranks of flyers carrying fresh bread in all the territories.

JULIUS: I want to bring back love songs, duets, old school style, like the way Motown changed the world with male and female couples singing songs that would melt away pain and inspire staying together through hard times.

(Pause)

Wait here, boss…I want you to hear something. There may be an answer… I'll be right back.

(Exit Julius, flying up to Audrey's apartment.)

JASMIN YASMIN LITTLEJOHN: Who would have known, viewers, that the notorious Donovan Wallinger III has a soft spot? And *Bird's View* revealed it first. Let's take a look at a new tweet:

Rhonda from the Bronx says: "You can sing on my stoop anytime Julius."

Julius is flying to Audrey's apartment. Let's follow him.

JULIUS: Hey, Mama.

(Pause)

You're too fly to not fly out of there. I'm Julius… And your name, my beauty?

BLOSSOM: Blossom.

JULIUS: And a lovely exotic bird flower you are. Time for you to get off that perch and come outside with me and the other pigeons.

BLOSSOM: (Looking outside)
    To the street? How is that a good time?

JULIUS: My beauty, this is where we congregate during
    the day. We have a rooftop bird penthouse in the
    next block. I'd like you to audition. My boss is
    considering opening a studio. I know you sing. You
    play the piano?

BLOSSOM: And I sing... Any style, but I have a
    fondness for love ballads.

JULIUS: (Sitting down at the piano and playing)
    A little small, but...

    (He sings and plays. Blossom joins in.)

BLOSSOM: That was amazing.

JULIUS: We were amazing.
    (Prepares to exit)
    What do you say? I see you're free to go. Come to
    the park and audition for my boss.

BLOSSOM: Yes... No... I'm domesticated... I don't
    think I can go to the park.

JULIUS: (Pointing out of the window)
    See that guy on the park bench? He's my boss.

BLOSSOM: I want to come with you, but...

JULIUS: That's my beauty, Blossom.

BLOSSOM: Are you married?

JULIUS: I'm going to be truthful with you. I've flown
    by your apartment before. I've been waiting for
    a chance to get close to you. I knew you were

different…special…someone I could…I could tell your voice was fantastic even though you sang such sad songs.

BLOSSOM: I could sing beautiful love songs with the right person.

JULIUS: You know what happens next…

BLOSSOM: I'm healing, from my last relationship…

JULIUS: We'll take our time.

AUDREY: I need to take care of Audrey. She owns this place, she's my people mate. Audrey was good to me until lately. She needs a steady love interest. What about your benefactor?

JULIUS: Anything for you. Donovan is single, a bird lover, and successful entrepreneur, but right now he is really interested in bread. Pigeon Carriers Unlimited, that's his company, but he's ready to try new things. Wave and smile. I'm going to go talk to him. I'll get him to come up to the apartment. See you soon.

(Julius exits through the window. Blossom waves and smiles at Donovan.
Enter Audrey through front door. She sets the oven on high and places a sheet of sunflower seeds inside.)

BLOSSOM: I have great news.

AUDREY: (Closing window)
I brought home some Brazilian sunflower seeds. Just wanted to get you a treat to say I'm sorry for the way I acted. Go check on the seeds and see if they are crispy enough.

BLOSSOM: Isn't that oven hot?

AUDREY: Just peck one…

(Blossom goes inside the oven to get a sunflower seed. Audrey closes the door. Blossom screams and thrashes around trying to get out. Knock on the door. Enter Donovan.)

DONOVAN WALLINGER III: Hello…I wanted to ask you about your bird.

JASMIN YASMIN LITTLEJOHN: Stay tuned to the next episode of "A Girl & Her Bird."

(Lights Out)

The End

KILL LESSON

Do I Have To?

Characters

Junior: Large adolescent male street cat, Killkeguard's son

Killkeguard: Adult male street cat, Junior's father

Susie: Small female domestic mouse

Setting

Present day. Afternoon. Alleyway on a restaurant row. Killkeguard is demonstrating kill movements. Junior is reading.

(Lights Rise)

KILLKEGUARD: It's all in the body, son. Our eyes innately show no fear. Your body communicates different intentions. When you're out for a kill your body needs to communicate to your prey: "Are you ready to die? I will assist you." It's all in the "Wait"

(Demonstrates)

"Stalk"

(Demonstrates)

and "Pounce"

(Demonstrates)

Then instinct takes over you chemically and you kill the sucker

(Demonstrates)

(Beat)

But it's no fun if you rely on instinct alone and don't intimidate your prey. That's how cats become fat and slow at an early age. They don't make an effort to nourish their killer instinct. I earned the name Killkeguard...guardian of the killer instinct. Devotion to killing every day.
Junior?

JUNIOR: (Still reading)
Yes Dad?

KILLKEGUARD: JUNIOR!

JUNIOR: Yes, Dad.

KILLKEGUARD: How did I earn my name Killkeguard?

JUNIOR: Aw...you were named after the Danish philosopher and social critic Kierkegaard?

KILLKEGUARD: Junior! Put those books away.

JUNIOR: Yes, Dad.

KILLKEGUARD: You're here for your kill lesson. Don't waste our time.

JUNIOR: (Holding up book)
Dad, let me show you something. These big cats:

lions, tigers, and panthers. All the same Latin family name for animals "Felidae." We're in the same family! Do you think we could go visit them...not in Sub Sahara Africa or Asia... In the Bronx, at the zoo?

KILLKEGUARD: No, we're not going to the zoo. Those big cats aren't interested in you.

JUNIOR: We've never been introduced.

KILLKEGUARD: Junior... You emotionally exhaust me more than killing subway rats. If you want to think about big cats as family, think about what you can learn from them.

(Reaching for the book)

Here's an example. This lion waits in the bush, focused, still...look at his body line...his front legs ready to run and pounce. His back legs ready to spring, handsome swagger...and here

(Pointing)

takes that zebra down, rips the torso to threads, all while enjoying his accomplishments.

JUNIOR: I think in that culture, the lioness usually hunts with other mothers, and the fathers stay home with the kids.

KILLKEGUARD: (Meow scream)

JUNIOR: Do you think the lion families in the Bronx miss hunting? They probably eat store-bought red meat.

KILLKEGUARD: If I hadn't promised your mother...

JUNIOR: I was reading that the big cats kill very large mammals like giraffes, and they can also kill people. Do street cats kill people?

KILLKEGUARD: Only in rare circumstances. We usually scratch them or rip their skin. Cats and people have unofficially agreed to coexist.

(Pause)

If only your mother could see my aggravation.

JUNIOR: Dad, I don't want to hear my birthing story again.

KILLKEGUARD: Most female cats have a litter of five or more young, but your mother had one kid--you. You were the biggest kitten we ever saw. Your eyes were closed, and you were chanting some Buddhist people chant.

JUNIOR: *Namu Amida Butsu*

KILLKEGUARD: Instead of abandoning you like most cat dads on the street, I'm working hard to train you. Junior, if you don't have kill skills, you've got no hope of survival out here. Kill first, or you will be killed.

JUNIOR: Dad...while you were talking about coexisting with people, I found these

(indicating in book)

white lions and white tigers with these people Siegfried and Roy...

KILLKEGUARD: Those are Las Vegas show cats... you can't compare us to show cats.

JUNIOR: Yes Dad.

KILLKEGUARD: (While exiting)

I'm gonna find some fish heads for our supper behind the Korean fish market. Show me some killer moves before I leave.

JUNIOR: Here's one…(dances hip hop). And I can do Michael Jackson from his video *Killer*.

(He demonstrates moves from the video *Thriller*)

KILLKEGUARD: It's *Thriller*, son.

(Pause)

I'll be back… There's a homeless guy that waits for the fish heads too. I wanna get there before he takes all of them. Greedy homeless people…

Try to kill something while I'm gone.

(Exit Killkeguard. As Junior is dancing, Susie enters.)

SUSIE: Hey.

JUNIOR: Hey.

SUSIE: I'm Susie.

JUNIOR: Junior.

(Pause)

You're a tiny mouse. You're cute.

SUSIE: Thanks.

JUNIOR: I've never seen you in the alley. What's up?

SUSIE: I'm not a street mouse, silly. I live in a townhouse over there. Snuck out while my Mom's sleeping.

JUNIOR: Is your mom forcing you to take kill lessons too?

SUSIE: I don't know what that is. My mom's made us kids go to hide & sneak lessons. We learned how to grab crumbs and run really fast so we aren't seen by people.

JUNIOR: Word? That's cool. I wouldn't mind learning something like that. I would give myself a superhero cat name like, "X Cat."

SUSIE: You could have a cartoon series named after you.

JUNIOR: Sweet. (While pacing)
Nice talking to you Susie, but I have to practice my kill moves before my Dad gets back. I don't want to disappoint him.

SUSIE: I understand. I don't like to disappoint my mother. I should be getting back to the townhouse.

JUNIOR: Would you look at a couple of my moves before you leave? I'd value your opinion.

SUSIE: Sure.

JUNIOR: Just let me know which one makes you feel the most scared.

(Junior demonstrates a move.)

SUSIE: Not scared.

(Junior demonstrates another move.)

SUSIE: I saw that video too.

(Junior demonstrates another move.)

SUSIE: You look really scary. It makes me feel too scared to move. Stop now. Okay?

(Enter Killkeguard)

KILLKEGUARD: Good, son. You have her in a good position. She can't run.

SUSIE: What are you doing, Junior? We're friends.

KILLKEGUARD: She's begging for her life. Enjoy the moment. Now kill.

(Junior hesitates. Susie cries and begs)

KILLKEGUARD (Cont'd): Kill her now, son.

(Junior hesitates)

KILLKEGUARD (Cont'd): Kill her!

JUNIOR: *Namu Amida Butsu*

(Imitating a pounce movement demonstrated by Killkeguard.)

(Susie screams as she is butchered to death.)

KILLKEGUARD: First kill. Just the beginning, son.

(Lights Out)
End of Play

VOICE LESSONS

Wishes to the Outside

Synopsis

"Voice Lessons" is the story of two celestial beings named HE and SHE who reside in a Caribbean utopia somewhere between heaven and earth. In exchange for the privilege of remaining together for eternity, they perform time-travel missions. Their responsibility is to collect lessons from the experiences of Africans in the diaspora that can help relieve the current suffering of the people. Once collected, they disperse the lessons as intentions that people feel as "inspiration." The story begins as they prepare to travel in time for the lessons of the day, the Voice Lessons.

Characters

HE: handsome Black man

SHE: beautiful Black woman

Setting

A hilltop in a Caribbean utopia. There is a coconut tree full of coconuts. HE is at the top of the tree with a cutlass, preparing to cut down a coconut. SHE stands at the bottom of the tree looking upward at HE.

(Lights)

SHE: Not that one, mon…go up more.

HE: Why me need go furdar. Dis one good. Dis ole piece here full of big ripe coconuts readi ta fall if me don't take dem way me self.

SHE: No, no, me say me wan de one en de top…de one close to de sky.

HE: Woman, why ya need trouble me so. Me kin cut down ten coconut n give ya all ya could use for one week or mor.

SHE: When ya be courtin me, ya climb up tree fardar den dis tree en ya cut down any coconut me choose.

HE: When me young me do lot of tings for de challenge, now me do wha necessary, en me say ya no need me climb all de way dere ta git de one coconut lookin at de sky.

SHE: No, me no need, but me wan. N en ya younga days ya git me wha me need n wha me want.

(He talks aloud to himself)

HE: En ya younga days, ya no fret so bout coconut.

SHE: Wha ya sayin?

HE: Me jis tinkin dat me need a betta cutlass ta git me sweetheart de coconut she wan.

SHE: Yeh, Yeh, me sure ya sayin dat.

(Pause)

It too late naw anyways. Come down. It time for de lesson.

(He climbs down from the tree. He places the cutlass on the ground next to the coconut tree. He picks up a food bag.)

HE: We got time ta feed ourselves first.

(He takes a sandwich from the lunch bag. She snatches it back and places it back in the food bag.)

HE: Wha?

SHE: Naw one morsel befor de lesson...ya know ya git gas afta de lesson if ya et right befor.

(He talks to himself.)

HE: No, is you give me bad stomach.

SHE: Ya takin bout me or at me?

HE: Me jis say, so nice ya always be concern bout me stomach...bein it so sensitive.

(He and She hold hands and gaze into each other's eyes. They look towards the sky together. Then they close their eyes.)

SHE: Wha ya feelin?

HE: Me not feelin any difference naw, but me feelin a change come soon.

SHE: Change? Me feelin big lesson coming. Lesson dat going ta have ta stay wit de people over long, long time.

HE: Big lesson…ya tink we make it back here safe?

(She strokes His face.)

SHE: We always do. No quittin dis job. Dis our pay fer de price of love.

(She and He embrace.)

SHE: Mo dan four hundred years, n de people still in need of de lessons.

HE: Can't stop the lessons.

(He and She sit on the ground under the coconut tree next to each other and begin to chant.)

HE & SHE: A mani mani mani mani mani mani…

(As the chanting becomes more intense, the tree magically disappears and the hilltop becomes an abyss. She and He time-travel to a woodland area between two farms in northern Virginia, 1858. He and She have become people in the time period—enslaved Africans. She stands up and arranges her clothing and head kerchief. She is looking around for He, who is not present in her view.)

SHE: I need to fix myself pretty. He always be sneakin away to see me. He don't even think about the danger. Slave masters and overseers always on the watch on the farm and the road nearby. Somehow He finds a way through the woods. Handsome, clever, and a voice I would recognize anywhere. Deep and strong and…

(She continues looking around for He.)

I just know He's going to come tonight cause the moon is full and bringing a lot of light for him to see through the bush. And when he comes, He's going to have a present. Because he always bring me a present. No matter present or not, I love him.

(He appears with his hands behind his back.)

SHE: I knew you'd come. I was hearing your voice in my head and thinking about what you would bring me.

HE: How you know I got something for you?

SHE: Cause ain't no other gal out here in these woods. And cause your hands behind your back. And cause you...

(She tries to grab His arms so that his hands will release what is inside.)

You...

(Playful arm struggle)

Always bring me...

(Playful arm struggle continues)

Something...

(She loses the struggle.)
(He hands She a bouquet of ferns from one hand.)

HE: Here's some lady ferns for you. These will soon wither and die.

(He takes a piece of cloth with a print on it from the knapsack. She puts down the bouquet of ferns to hold the cloth with two hands.)

HE: Here's some lady ferns for you printed on cloth. These ferns will live as long as the cloth lives.

SHE: How did you get the green color and the fern picture on the cloth? It looks so real.

HE: I make a dye from the plants, and I made a print. In my home my grandfather and my father made the prints on the cloth, and they taught me. I did it a new way here. A new way for this new place. Dying and printing remind me of home and now this cloth will remind you of me. The print is my voice on cloth.

(Sounds of people walking and dogs in the woods)

HE: I best be leaving now before the master does the head count.

SHE: I'm going to hide this cloth and keep it forever.

HE: That may be a promise this place won't let you keep. Goodnight my lady. Put my voice under your head and sleep sweetly.

(He and She run in opposite directions. She has the knapsack with the cloth. The bouquet of ferns remains on the ground. The sounds of dogs and slave catchers intensifies. He disappears in the darkness. She stops running.)

SHE: My green ferns.

(She starts to run back through the woods to retrieve the ferns. The sounds of dogs and slave catchers intensify. She picks up the ferns and then hides in the bushes as the sounds of the dogs and slave catchers reach a crescendo.)

SHE: I see dem coming fast. Dey found you out. Hide.

(Sounds of slave catchers beating He. He screams from agony and pain. Sounds of dogs biting and chewing on

His flesh. Wails of She as she watches the beating in the distance and hears the sound of His voice.)

HE: My legs... No more master...not my face...

(Sound of H being dragged away. Dogs are silent. Low mutters of slave catchers as they move further and further away.)

SHE: He didn't harm nobody. He wasn't running... He was going back. We just wanted to be together. He came to see me.

(Pause)

Will I ever hear your voice again?

(The abyss is transformed into a contemporary kindergarten classroom. The classroom is modest with very little furnishings and very little equipment and supplies. However, signs of children's creativity are everywhere. He and She are inhabited by the spirits of five-year-old children. She is singing a playful improvised song without the regularity of an adult composed song and dancing.)

SHE: Pop, pop, popcorn

I'm making the

Pop popcorn

Get a big pot

Stir it up, stir it up

Put in the grease

Stir it up, stir it up

Put it on the stove.

Make the fire big and hot

(Spoken)

When your Mommy can't see you.

(Singing resumes)

Stir it up, stir it up

Then watch it pop

Do the popcorn dance

Stir it up, stir it up

Pop pop

Do the popcorn dance

Stir it up, Stir it up

Pop, pop

HE: Stop that singing.

SHE: I don't have to stop. You're not the boss of my voice.

HE: Stop...That's not a real song. You made it up.

SHE: It's a real song, and I made it up, so it's a real song.

(Singing and dancing resumes)

Stir it up. Stir it up.

(He cries hysterically)

SHE: Why you crying? It's just a popcorn song and my popcorn dance.

(He speaks unintelligible word like sounds.)

SHE: Use your words. Use your voice. I can't understand you.

(He responds through exaggerated audible breathing.)

HE: Green. I need more green crayons. I only have forest green. I need more colors. I need fern green and jungle green, and pine green, and emerald green… I want to finish my story.

(He holds up construction paper with green scribbles.)

SHE: What does that say?

(He stops crying as he begins to enthusiastically tell his story. He points to the lines on the paper as if they are real words.)

The green dragon with five heads was walking into the castle where the princess was hiding, and he was huffing and puffing. I'll blow your house down said the big bad wolf, and the African prince heard the Brooklyn princess scream save me save me. I'll protect you. What big eyes you have, said the wolf, and the prince called his magic dogs from the playground. Growl, growl. And the magic dogs cooked the pancakes and…

(He pulls out the green crayon and scribbles more as if writing real words.)

I forgot a part.

(He puts the crayon away and begins to "read" again.)

The first dragonhead was the greediest, and he tried to eat up all the pancakes, but the very smart African prince who looked like me said, no, you need to share, and all the dragonheads ate the pancakes, and it was a trick…

(He turns the paper over and reads the reverse side of the paper.)

…and the dragonheads and the dragon bodies started to shrink until they got very small, like smaller than a bug, and then they couldn't hurt the Brooklyn princess from Fulton Street, and she was so happy, and she said to the handsome very smart African prince who looks like me, my hero superman, and the African prince superman hero and the princess from Atlantic Avenue…

(He takes out the crayon and makes a correction on the paper.)

…the princess from Fulton Street went together with the magic dogs who are very good dogs and went to the store and got free ice cream without preservatives. The End.

(She claps enthusiastically.)

SHE: That's a good story. I liked your voices. You don't need any more crayons.

HE: Yes I do… It's my vision…

(Pause)

When I get big, I'm gonna make bigger and bigger stories with bigger and bigger voices.

(Pause)

HE: I like your popcorn song and your popcorn dance.

SHE: I know… When I get big, I'm gonna make more dances and more songs. I gonna make a song about…potato chips.

(SHE sings)

Take a handful out the bag and crunch crunch crunch.

(SHE whispers to HE)

SHE: And I don't use the stove. I'm too little. I use my imagination.

(The kindergarten transforms back into an abyss. The abyss becomes a psychiatric ward in a public hospital. She is pacing back and forth in front of a chair. She is wearing a nightgown. One side of She's face is deformed from assaults and burns.)

SHE: I had a voice once. An outside voice that other people could hear. Now I only have an inside voice…

(She rubs her chest)

Somewhere in here. I can feel it… I feel all the time that it wants to get out. But it's stuck. How long has it been stuck… Since they took my face. I stand in front of the bathroom mirror. I say… move mouth…talk…nobody is around…if you're afraid to come out it's safe now…no one else can hear you…just me…I would like to hear what my own voice sounds like again. I was tickling myself, in the smooth places of my armpits. I thought I could get myself to laugh or at least smile. I heard the doctor tell the nurse that the pills would stop my meaningless repetitive behavior. Don't you understand? I have meaning. It's in here.

(She reenacts a beating disfiguring her face.)

My legs… I can't feel my legs anymore… Not my face… Don't beat my face. I wasn't hurting anybody. I was walking home. Look what you did to my face…my face… It's burning, it's burning.

(Pause)

Come out, voice… Help me tell them that I'm hurting. Help me tell them I've crawled up inside myself because I don't know what else to do. Voice, don't you remember how in the past we used to sing silly silly songs, made no sense at all. It was fun. Let's have fun together again, voice. I need you.

(She sits on a chair and stares blankly into space. He enters. He is dressed in contemporary clothes. He is holding a magazine, a bag of popcorn, and a bouquet of green ferns.)

HE: How are you doing today, princess? Looking beautiful as ever. I'm not ignoring what they did to you… You have a new beauty now. Try to look at me, please. After all this time I'm not going to ask you to talk to me. Don't want to impose. I'm going to just think of this as your artistic silent period… Like all the geniuses have their periods of this and their periods of that… Can you look at me, princess?

(Pause)

I'm selfish. Maybe you're perfectly content inside that pretty head of yours. But I need to hear your voice for me. I miss your voice. When we were little, you still had that squeaky kindergarten voice. I know the truth is you want to stay inside because you're hurting. You pulled that pain in. …

(Pause)

Presents. Do you remember how I used to be obsessed over the color green----still am. I saw these beautiful green ferns as I was walking up the path. I think they're called lady ferns… Weeds to most people… I thought you would like them.

(He gives She the ferns and then shows the magazine.)

My first publication. Finally, a publisher took a chance on me. Funny…I'm sharing my voice on paper while I'm trying to get you to share your voice in any way again. I told you when we were in kindergarten that I was going to write big stories. You said you were going to write songs and make dances. We kept our promises to each other and ourselves. It doesn't have to end for you. Let your hurt come out in your songs and your dance. Perform the hell out of your hurt. Share your inside with the outside.

(He strokes She's face)

My lady, my beautiful lady… I didn't have a chance to protect you… You were coming home…coming to me…not hurting anybody… Vicious and cruel…senseless… Will it ever stop?

(Pause)

One last thing before I leave you…microwave popcorn…still warm. I know you remember that silly popcorn song you used to sing.

(He attempts to sing the popcorn song and do the popcorn dance in order to get She's attention. He doesn't remember the song or dance well.)

Stir it up, stir it up

Then watch it pop

Do the popcorn dance

Stir it up, stir it up

Pop pop

(He gives up his singing and dancing attempt)

HE: Thought I could at least get a laugh.

(Pause)

They're going to start kicking the visitors out in a few minutes. I'll be back tomorrow. I'm not giving up. You can't give up either. I'll be your voice until you're ready. You fight to come out. I'll fight to come in.

(He exits. She begins to sing.)

SHE: Pop, pop, popcorn

I'm making the

Pop pop popcorn

Get a big pot

Stir it up, stir it up

(The abyss appears. He has returned to his original persona in the Caribbean utopia. She remains in trance with her last time-traveled experience. He shakes her to help her retrieve her spirit.)

HE: Wha de lesson?

Wha de lesson?

Ya mus say de lesson so ya kin come back.

Ya mus come back, me need ya come back.

SHE: Share your inside with the outside.

HE & SHE: Share your inside with the outside.

(Stars appear all around He and She. They gather the stars which represent intentions that will become inspiration and put them in the knapsack. They hold the knapsack together and cast the stars out on the people. The hilltop and the coconut tree return. He looks toward the top of the tree..)

SHE: It hard com back dis time.

HE: Me sweatin, tinkin maybe ya not come back to me.

SHE: Big work need big time. Like gittin dat coconut up dere.

HE: Ya still wan it, de coconut look at de sky. Ya know me git it fer ya, my sweet.

SHE: Naw, me no need. Me jis like fer ya ta say ya do it. Make me feel special.

(He and She sit on the hilltop. She takes the sandwich out of the food bag. He and She share the sandwich.)

SHE: Who take a bite of dis?

HE: Big job...big appetite. Me git a taste while me wait fer ya come back ta me.

(He and She embrace)

(Lights Out)

End of Play

About the Author

Cesi (Cecelia) Davidson holds a doctorate degree in Speech Language Hearing Sciences from the Graduate School and University Center of the City University of New York. She has provided therapeutic services for children with communication and learning challenges for over thirty years. Playwriting emerged after years of dialogue as a therapist, mother, sister, friend, companion, and periods of spiritual introspection. She reimagined her experiences in order to create compelling stories for the stage, giving voice to her witness of human suffering and triumphs. Since beginning to write in 2009, she has written hundreds of plays demonstrating a broad range, fearless creativity, and cultural responsiveness. Her writing includes humorous explorations of personified objects to horrific stories of incest. Cesi is a producing artist. She's founder and curator of Short Plays to Nourish the Mind & Soul, free public theatre in New York City. Cesi is one of eight siblings, and the mother of two outstanding young men, Hannibal and Rahakmah Bryan. She is in a devoted relationship with her partner Edward Feeney.